STRENGTH
in the *River*

Lessons in Hope from
Suffering Saints of the Bible

STEVE SWARTZ

KRESS
BIBLICAL
RESOURCES

Kress Biblical Resources
The Woodlands, Texas
www.kressbiblical.com

ISBN: 978-1-934952-26-9

Dedication

This book is dedicated to you who read –
to the Jeremiahs and Jobs whose tears are fresh.
May God be glorified in your lives as His strong, right hand
upholds you even as the floods rise. May this journey of
understanding God's faithfulness give you
strength in your river.

- S. S. -

Thanks

Many thanks to Emily Moore and Heather Olewiler
for their countless hours of help without which
Strength in the River would not exist. May your efforts bear
fruit in the lives of precious believers for many years to come.
Thanks also to Sam Moore, Cathy Bloxham, and my wife, Sylvia,
for their detailed editing and suggestions.

I am further indebted to my wife, Sylvia,
who provided the original inspiration for this book.
She has waded through many rivers of tears,
some that no one but she and I know. She has always
sought after the Lord no matter how deep the waters get.

I am most grateful to our glorious God who plots our
courses that include valleys of the shadow of death,
but we will fear no evil. His ways are far above our ways
and His thoughts far above our thoughts.

Contents

Foreword

Too many Christian books and blogs dealing with suffering offer only platitudes and anecdotes devoid of the stability of substantial truth. *Strength in the River* is a notable exception because of its careful and caring exposition of the enduring truth of Scripture. Steve Swartz avoids abstract theological reflection by taking you into the daily lives of biblical men and women, carefully unfolding their excruciating experience with suffering, and practically illustrates how you should respond to adversity. It is immensely practical and biblical.

Scripture is filled with examples of suffering saints who illustrate the truth that disease, destruction, and death are the great teachers about life (Ecclesiastes 7:1-5). To an even greater extent, the Bible shows you how to endure through these trials. "For whatever was written in earlier times was written for our instruction, so that through perseverance and the encouragement of the Scriptures we might have hope" (Romans 15:4, NASV). *Strength in the River* goes to the chief resource for your hope in the midst of your suffering, God's Word, and demonstrates practically how you can persevere. The great English preacher of the nineteenth century, Charles Spurgeon, wrote: "I have learned to kiss the wave that throws me against the Rock of Ages." Can you do that when you are experiencing God's severe providence? This book will help you learn!

Dr. John D. Street
July 30, 2016

1

A River of Tears:
When the Pain Will Not Stop

"*D*ad was killed." These were the concluding words in my brother's tear-filled phone call to me early on a cool February morning. A teenage driver had crossed four lanes of traffic and hit Dad's car head-on, killing him instantly and critically injuring our stepmother. The emotional detonation that happens in the mind and heart at that moment, the same experience being suffered by my brother and our other family members, defies description. One minute before that phone call, I had just finished packing for a family camping trip to begin later that day. Now, the fabric of life had been torn permanently as the rising tide of disbelief, shock, and growing agony began to flood my heart.

I went into our bedroom where my wife was still sleeping. She was so close to my father. I didn't want to awaken her. I knew the explosion of pain that must come to her now. After telling her the news, we wept together for a time. We reluctantly gathered our children together to tell them that their grandpa had died. And now, instead of hopping in the van to enjoy camping together, we had to unpack all the camping equipment and re-pack as quickly as we could to drive the eight hours to where my stepmother was hospitalized.

When the Pain First Arrives

When the pain of a life-altering event first arrives, the theological truths about God and suffering we have learned from Scripture carry us, which is why a secure grounding in the faithful character of God is so important. But at that *actual moment* and in the days and weeks to follow, the ability to grasp and learn new truth is in large part overwhelmed by grief. And theological truths expressed in the form of pithy clichés or platitudes can not only be unhelpful but also thoroughly insensitive.

Less than an hour after my dad's death, a well-meaning friend told me unoriginally, "Well, at least he's in a better place." Yes, my dad loved the Lord Jesus Christ and as a born-again Christian was most assuredly in heaven with God Himself. But at that moment, I didn't *want* my dad in heaven. I *wanted* him here! I wanted to tell him *I loved him*! I wanted to *embrace him*! I wanted to tell him that I wasn't *ready* for this! I even wanted to ask him, "What do I *do*, Dad? How do I *handle this*?" The very one I needed to talk to was the one who had died! My family and I didn't need my friend to tell us some obvious truth; we needed him to *mourn* with us.

As we arrived late that night at the hospital, my dear grieving and injured stepmother affirmed her continued trust and faith in the Lord. But she didn't need "10 Reasons Why Heaven is Better than Earth." She needed to hold hands. She needed to be surrounded by people, the earthly hands of God, to grieve and cry with her. She needed people to pray for her and over her, crying out to God in stark agony on her behalf.

If this book has made its way into your hands and this is the place in which you find yourself, the immediate distress and grief of a dark surprise trial—then perhaps it is too soon for *Strength in the River*. You don't need words on paper as much as you need prayer, friends, and lots of boxes of tissue. You are on emotional life-support and need time to regain some sense of equilibrium. Just gently put the book next to your bed and know that it will be there when you are ready.

When the Pain Will Not Stop

For some, suffering may be the result of a clearly definable event—the loss of a loved one, a serious or chronic health concern, the rebellion of a wayward child. For others, suffering may come in the form of a mysterious depression that seems to defy your trust in the Lord and has no observable cause. Whatever the origin, you may reach a point when you thought that the hurt was *supposed* to start decreasing, but it is not. The pain will not stop. It is at this point that you begin to realize that you are no longer in a short-term crisis so much as a marathon of endurance, a swollen river of grief, a *river made of your own tears,* that seems as if it will never subside.

This is the point at which it is my prayer that *Strength in the River* has found its way into your hands. The river of pain is not receding so you need spiritual strength with which to withstand the powerful current. Your mind is able to grasp weighty truths from Scripture and your heart is ready to receive it. The Lord has graciously brought you through the initial crisis, but now you need to begin a journey through the long-term implications of your situation.

When your crisis first arrived, you most desperately needed the immediate prayers and practical support of friends and family. Now, we turn together to receive comfort from friends who have gone before us, companions from the pages of Scripture. If you have trusted Christ as your Savior, turning away from your love of sin and turning to the free gift of forgiveness offered by God in Christ, then most assuredly the people of whom you will read in these pages are your friends as well.

God did not inspire the Bible as some sort of dry theological essay. For much of the Bible, truth is presented in story form, the real-life accounts of men and women who trusted the Lord in varying degrees. Some, like Ruth, stand as a shining example of grace under pressure. Others, like David, have rougher edges at times. But all highlight the fact that God is faithful, God is true, and God is compassionate. The very fact that these men and women are recorded in God's inspired Scripture demonstrates that God completely understands human pain and has answers for our suffering.

Beginning the Journey

The prophet Jeremiah experienced great grief at the destruction of his country. The southern Israelite kingdom of Judah was slowly disintegrating, such that Jerusalem and the surrounding area were rendered absolutely unusable—trees cut down, crops burned, and cities leveled. The Babylonians finished their devastating work in 586 BC.

Jerusalem is the capital city of the Bible. It is the geographical focus of Scripture and the central place of worship for the Jew. In Bible times, one could meet with God at the city temple and offer various sacrifices. In fact, Jerusalem was so closely identified with Israel that it was commonly called the "daughter" of Israel. It was a representation of God's blessing upon Israel. God's chosen people were the Israelites, and God's chosen city was Jerusalem.

Jeremiah watched in horror as his beloved land crumbled during this national crisis. So strong was his love and so genuine his concern for Judah that he was called the "weeping prophet." He wrote that **"my eyes flow with rivers of tears because of the destruction of the daughter of my people" (Lam 3:48).** But the southern Israelite kings of Judah rebelled against God. Their disobedience would eventually lead to the utter destruction of Jerusalem. It was a devastating event that could have been prevented by repentance, but Jeremiah watched as over a period of years Judah was slowly dismantled, stone by stone. Jeremiah was grieved to tears as their hearts hardened more and more; he wept and became depressed over the state of his nation.

You've known what it means for your eyes to flow with rivers of tears—for the torrent of pain, disappointment, and suffering to overwhelm you. Grief can be so sudden and so shocking that it literally devastates your health, mental well-being, and even your ability to think straight. In a matter of minutes, a perfectly intelligent Christian can become mentally paralyzed, unable to focus enough to make basic decisions. This is a river promised by Jesus Christ Himself. He does not promise a utopic land of fantasy, but instead gives a rather unexpected promise in John 16:33, "In the world you *will* have tribulation" (emphasis added).

The point is this: we all wade through rivers of tears, but the Lord uses these very rivers to conform us to the image of His Son. They are a gift from the Lord. They may be hard and painful, but they are necessary. Ultimately, we know they are valuable and that they bring peace. The river may be deep and dark and take supernatural fortitude to navigate, but once we are on the other side of that river, we realize that we wouldn't have traded it for anything because of the spiritual value of the trial.

So we're going to go to Scripture and invite the Lord Jesus and precious believers from all ages of Scripture—from the creation of man to the apostles of the New Testament—to a round-table discussion. These believers all greatly suffered and trusted the Lord in the midst of their rivers. They each have a lesson for us to learn, words of wisdom and counsel to trust God which we can apply to our own situations. We will be hearing from Jesus Himself, Jeremiah, James, Abraham, Ruth, Paul, David (on two occasions), Peter, Elijah, Job, Eve, Heman, Joseph, and Hannah. Each lesson will help us build spiritual muscle and "strength in the river." It is my prayer that when you are finished, God is bigger and your faith stronger.

2

Jeremiah Says,
"Accept That God's Sovereignty
is Bigger Than You Think"

The foundation for victoriously walking through suffering must be the doctrine of the sovereignty of God. Our understanding of God's sovereignty directly impacts the level of joy we will experience and should grow into a robust, mighty pillar of strength in our hearts. Jeremiah introduces us to this important lesson to gain victory in the midst of pain.

Israel's Situation

Sin was rampant. Apostasy continued. When Jerusalem fell to the Babylonians in 586 BC, Israel understood that their own sin was to blame. Jeremiah, a prophet of the Lord, wrote of this great suffering, "Her foes have become the head; her enemies prosper, because the LORD has afflicted her for the multitude of her transgressions; her children have gone away, captives before the foe" (Lam 1:5).

In 605 BC the powerful Nebuchadnezzar, king of Babylon, made Jehoiakim, king of Judah, his servant for three years. He placed Jerusalem as a vassal city under Babylon and took home captives, among whom was Daniel. When Jehoiakim finally rebelled, Nebuchadnezzar formed an alliance of Chaldeans, Moabites, and Ammonites against Judah and thoroughly thrashed Jerusalem to teach them a lesson.

About eight years later, 18-year-old Jehoiachin reigned as king of Judah for just three months before surrendering to Nebuchadnezzar. Babylon captured most of Judah's inhabitants and installed a puppet king, Zedekiah, to do Babylon's bidding. But Zedekiah planned a rebellion with the surrounding cities and nations of Edom, Moab, Ammon, Tyre, and Sidon, possibly even trying to get Egypt to help as well. Zedekiah was summoned to Babylon to explain himself, and although he somehow weaseled his way out, the king's suspicion was aroused.

Nebuchadnezzar marched into Judah, laying Jerusalem under siege. Meanwhile, Jeremiah was prophesying to King Zedekiah, telling him that the Lord would give their city over to Babylon. Furious with this news, Zedekiah threw Jeremiah in prison, despite the siege. Nebuchadnezzar turned his full fury upon Jerusalem, starving its citizens to death by cutting off their food supply. Finally, Zedekiah led his army in an inspiring run for their lives in the middle of the night, but the Babylonian army overtook them near Jericho. They forced Zedekiah to watch the execution of his own sons, then blinded him and brought him to Babylon, imprisoning him in chains until death.

Unfortunately, during this grueling time of national suffering, the kings of Judah missed the entire point of their trial from God. The problem was *not* Babylon. The problem was their own faithlessness to God and their abandonment of the Mosaic Covenant they had promised to faithfully keep. As a result of their disobedience, countless lives were lost and others radically altered in captivity.

The Sovereignty of God

How we handle suffering is directly related to our view of God. Most professing Christians think they believe in the sovereign power of God, but in reality they don't act like they believe that God is *completely* sovereign. They don't believe God is in control of every single event in their life.

However, God does not react—except in situations divinely orchestrated that He would, such as answering prayer and saving the repentant. And yet even these events are still foreordained. The Bible never says that we have freedom outside of God's control. Although we do have freedom to make real choices with real consequences, we can never do anything outside of the sovereign purview of God.

Now we'll hit closer to home. What about the suffering Christian who immediately responds to a trial with anger toward God? This reveals an attitude that says, "God does *not* know what He is doing!" Or what about the suffering Christian who believes himself to be the center of God's plan and will not be joyful until his problem is resolved? Or who feels entitled to view himself as a victim and believes that "Precious Me" should not have to go through this? Or who believes that he deserves more or merits better treatment? Or who believes that the gospel of Christ is not sufficient comfort for suffering?

So my question is this: do we *really* believe in the sovereignty of God? Based on this list many of us would be eliminated. We need to listen to the counsel of Jeremiah that says, "Accept that God's sovereignty is bigger than you think." We need to expand our view of God's sovereignty. We need to recognize three facts about God: He is accountable to no one, He is not our pawn, and He will rectify all things.

God is Accountable to No One

Jeremiah, representing the affliction of Jerusalem, described what God had done, "I am the man who has seen affliction under the rod of his wrath; he has driven and brought me into darkness without any light; surely against me he turns his hand again and again the whole day long" (Lam 3:1-3). Instead of enjoying the light of God's loving guidance, Jeremiah lived in darkness without direction and without hope. The loving hand of God was clenched into a fist of fury, relentlessly striking him over and over. Jeremiah wrote of long starvation and the weakness which results, "He has made my flesh and my skin waste away; he has broken my bones" (3:4).

The suffering and darkness was not only physical but also emotional. "He has besieged and enveloped me with bitterness and tribulation; he has made me dwell in darkness like the dead of long ago" (3:5-6). Suffering overwhelmed him to the point of feeling useless and dead.

We often repeat the familiar phrase, "Take it to the Lord in prayer" and believe God will fix all our problems if we ask Him. But what if, in His predetermined plan, He is *not* going to do what we ask? What if God planned your trial for a purpose, and the journey of anguish is going to happen no matter what? What if the river is only going to rise higher? Jeremiah recognized that there was nothing he could do to thwart God's will, "He has walled me about so that I cannot escape; he has made my chains heavy; though I call and cry for help, he shuts out my prayer; he has blocked my ways with blocks of stones; he has made my paths crooked" (3:7-8).

God did not answer Jeremiah's prayer. Instead, He was the very one who *determined* Jerusalem's destruction. God was the divine hunter, and Jerusalem was His prey. He planned to do harm, "He is a bear lying in wait for me, a lion in hiding" (3:10); "He turned aside my steps and tore me to pieces; he has made me desolate" (3:11); "He bent his bow and set me as a target for his arrow" (3:12); "He drove into my kidneys the arrows of his quiver" (3:13). God carried out this harm like a vicious beast, an expert archer.

As if physical decimation wasn't enough, humiliation was unbearable, "I have become the laughingstock of all peoples, the object of their taunts all day long" (3:14). Jerusalem had become the object of derision and the joke of other nations. "All who pass along the way clap their hands at you; they hiss and wag their heads at the daughter of Jerusalem: 'Is this the city that was called the perfection of beauty, the joy of all the earth?'" (2:15).

Besides national humiliation, Jeremiah was personally disgraced. In Jeremiah 20, he complained that his prophecies were ridiculed and no one believed him, "O LORD, you have deceived me, and I was deceived; you are stronger than I, and you have prevailed. I have become a laughingstock all the day; everyone mocks me" (Jer 20:7). Even when the prophecies came true, Jeremiah was still taunted by his fellow Jews.

Jeremiah was left with a never-ending sorrow, "He has filled me with bitterness; he has sated me with wormwood" (Lam 3:15). Wormwood is a small shrub with a bitter taste used to purge the body of impurities. Every biblical reference to it is a metaphor for bitterness and sorrow, and this was no exception.

As a representation of his personal sorrow, as well as that of Jerusalem, Jeremiah was utterly demeaned and demoralized by God, "He has made my teeth grind on gravel, and made me cower in ashes" (3:16). His plight was like that of someone's face being forced to the ground in gravel and rocks with such force that his teeth break, and he is further thrown onto a heap of ashes to curl up in fear and agony.

Jeremiah was now just a shadow of the man he used to be. There was no serenity, no cheerfulness, no strength left in him at all. He was entirely broken. "My soul is bereft of peace; I have forgotten what happiness is; so I say, 'My endurance has perished; so has my hope from the LORD'" (3:17-18). All he could think about was how miserable he was and how hopeless Jerusalem looked as it smoldered after the devastating obliteration by Nebuchadnezzar's army. The prophet's mind was obsessed with suffering, "Remember my affliction and my wanderings, the wormwood and the gall! My soul continually remembers it and is bowed down within me" (3:19-20).

Jeremiah expressed feelings of distance and detachment. He didn't call God by name for the first seventeen verses of his lament. God was the distant "He" and "Him." When he did bring up the name of "the LORD" in Lamentations 3:18, God's name was just a distant memory of what used to be. Jeremiah was essentially saying, "I *used to* have hope in the Lord, but now He is afflicting me."

Putting ourselves into perspective, does this sound like God asked anyone's permission to allow or inflict suffering? Does God need to read the latest blog on human ethics to try to rehabilitate His image? Does God need a spin doctor to put Him in a kinder, gentler light? Or does this picture of God take your breath away and put you face to face with a God who does what He pleases, when He pleases, for His own reasons?

Jerusalem had been sinning for generations and was finally being judged, but somehow Jeremiah got thrown in the suffering as well! This suffering wasn't based on the discipline of the Lord, but it wasn't unexplained suffering either. We know exactly where it came from and why.

Sometimes it's tempting to treat God as if *He* is somehow accountable to *us*. "Lord, this is *really* crossing the line now! This is too much!" we complain. Instead, we need to recognize, "Lord, I tremble at Your might and Your power, and You have all authority to snuff me out and inflict all sorts of mysterious pains and difficulties. You are *not* accountable to anyone, and I acknowledge Your complete charge over all things!"

God is Not Our Pawn

The second fact to expand our view of God's sovereignty is that God is not our pawn. Lamentations 3:43-44 reads, "You have wrapped yourself with anger and pursued us, killing without pity; you have wrapped yourself with a cloud so that no prayer can pass through." God was chastening His people; He was determined to see pain carried to its climax. How many prayers do you think were offered up during this siege? What about during the final battle? How many cries for help? God was silent and let it happen. There was no divine rescue given to the Israelites.

The results were overwhelming. Israel and Judah essentially ceased to exist in the minds of other nations. Jeremiah writes, "You have made us scum and garbage among the peoples. All our enemies open their mouths against us; panic and pitfall have come upon us, devastation and destruction'" (Lam 3:45-46). The nation had fallen apart, and was a complete failure. This was heartbreak on the level of the Holocaust. Jeremiah plunged into deep sorrow after witnessing starvation, rape, murder, and what felt like hell on earth. He cried, "My eyes flow with rivers of tears because of the destruction of the daughter of my people. My eyes will flow without ceasing, without respite, until the LORD from heaven looks down and sees; my eyes cause me grief at the fate of all the daughters of my city" (3:48-51).

It became clear to Jeremiah that God was not at the beck and call of man. He was not a man to be tested or manipulated. Clearly, God was moving in terrifying ways. But what was Jeremiah's conclusion? "Let us test and examine our ways, and return to the LORD! Let us lift up our hearts and hands to God in heaven: 'We have transgressed and rebelled, and you have not forgiven'" (3:40-42). Jeremiah used this suffering as an opportunity to examine his own heart and to purify his own faith.

We must remember that God is not a divine "Get Out of Jail Free" card, nor a heavenly genie to keep us from breaking a nail or shedding a tear. He is under no obligation to meet our expectations concerning our prayers, how He expresses His for love us, or to the manner of His help in time of need.

Consider this illustration: the wife of a famous television preacher wrote in an article for Focus on the Family, "Each day, before I drop our kids off at school, we hold hands and pray for the school, their teachers and friends. I speak words of blessing over them, telling them, 'You have the favor of God.'"ii This sounds innocuous enough, but it is centered in a belief that God is beholden to *my* words.

Suffering and trials act like windshield wipers to clear the fog off your view of God. The awesome might and greatness of God comes into focus more than ever when you begin to realize that you don't have an ounce of control over what is happening! In Job 10:8-9, Job writes, "Your hands fashioned and made me, and now you have destroyed me altogether. Remember that you have made me like clay; and will you return me to the dust?"

God Rectifies All Things

Now take a deep breath. We must stop and remember that God rectifies all things. He puts *everything* right! It was in God's sovereign purpose to elevate Babylon and allow the Chaldeans to destroy Jerusalem because of Judah's sin. Yet it was also in God's plan to take vengeance on Babylon for daring to mess with His beloved Israel!

In Lamentations 3:52-66 we see the transition from despair to hope, from miserable brokenness to complete restoration:

> I have been hunted like a bird by those who were my enemies
> without cause; they flung me alive into the pit and cast stones
> on me; water closed over my head; I said, "I am lost." I called

on your name, O LORD, from the depths of the pit; you heard my plea, "Do not close your ear to my cry for help!" You came near when I called on you; you said, "Do not fear!" You have taken up my cause, O LORD; you have redeemed my life. You have seen the wrong done to me, O LORD; judge my cause. You have seen all their vengeance, all their plots against me. You have heard their taunts, O LORD, all their plots against me. The lips and thoughts of my assailants are against me all the day long. Behold their sitting and their rising; I am the object of their taunts. You will repay them, O LORD, according to the work of their hands. You will give them dullness of heart; your curse will be on them. You will pursue them in anger and destroy them from under your heavens, O LORD.

Jeremiah writes that God will repay them. This is more of a request than a statement of fact. Jeremiah pleads, "Please repay the Babylonians for their evil deeds!" In payment for their sin, God curses them, destroys them, and gives them a dull heart and an inability to repent. Jeremiah 51:11 clearly states that God is the one who would do this, "The LORD has stirred up the spirit of the kings of the Medes, because his purpose concerning Babylon is to destroy it, for that is the vengeance of the LORD, the vengeance for his temple." This is so instructive for us today! Suffering and pain are *never* without purpose. They are *never* without cause. For the believer in Christ, suffering and pain *never* happen without eventual resolution!

While in prison at Rome, the apostle Paul expressed full confidence that the Lord would bring perfect resolution to his trial, that God would vindicate him, and that Christ would be honored. He put a small qualifier at the end of his statement in Philippians 1:19-20, "For I know that through your prayers and the help of the Spirit of Jesus Christ this will turn out for my deliverance, as it is my eager expectation and hope that I will not be at all ashamed, but that with full courage now as always Christ will be honored in my body, *whether by life or by death*" (emphasis added).

Let's establish this point: most of the time God will *not* resolve your suffering *when* you want Him to, *but* 100% of the time God *will* resolve your suffering! Can you see that our faulty picture of a little convenient God is nothing more than a churchified candy machine? Can you see that God has big purposes, much bigger than you, and that His whole existence does *not* revolve around you? God is surely higher and mightier in your mind than He was a few minutes ago!

Four Responses to a Hope-Expanded View of God's Sovereignty

How do we respond to this understanding of God's sovereignty? First, *I need to hope in God's mercy.* Yes, God does what He wants when He wants. Yes, pain and suffering can come in a way we least want it to come. But God is kind and merciful. In Lamentations 3:21 Jeremiah reminds himself of how he should think, "But this I call to mind, and therefore I have hope." What gives him hope? The next two verses read, "The steadfast love of the LORD never ceases; his mercies never come to an end; they are new every morning; great is your faithfulness" (Lam 3:22-23).

Your trial is not the barometer of whether or not God loves you at that particular moment. God has already proven His love for you. Romans 5:8 states, "But God shows his love for us in that while we were still sinners, Christ died for us." Just because you are enduring a trial doesn't mean that God's mercy is on hold. His mercy is still active! Every single morning His mercy continues on like clockwork. In fact, Jeremiah disciplines himself to think the right thoughts. He writes, "'The LORD is my portion,' says my soul, 'therefore I will hope in him'" (Lam 3:24). A "portion" is a share of something, an inheritance. Jeremiah is saying, "My inheritance is with the LORD! I belong to Him!"

Second, *I am to wait on God's timing.* People say in the midst of suffering, "I just don't know what to do!" Let's see what Jeremiah says to do. "The LORD is good to those who wait for him, to the soul who seeks him. It is good that one should wait quietly for the salvation of the LORD. It is good for a man that he bear the yoke in his youth" (3:25-27). Three times Jeremiah says that it is *good* to wait.

This goes against our conventional wisdom that says, "I *hate* waiting!" Instead, Jeremiah says, "It is *good* to wait!" We need to use this time to seek the Lord and make a conscious decision to wait without complaint. As we bear the yoke of suffering in our youth, we learn and grow in strength! We are reminded in James 1:2-3 to "Count it all joy, my brothers, when you meet trials of various kinds, for you know that the testing of your faith produces steadfastness."

Third, *I am to submit to God's plan*. Submission is such a key element in responding to suffering that we will spend an entire chapter on it later, but it is also a key response to recognizing God's sovereignty. Lamentations 3:28-30 reads, "Let him sit alone in silence when it is laid on him; let him put his mouth in the dust—there may yet be hope; let him give his cheek to the one who strikes, and let him be filled with insults."

There is no resistance, no bitterness. There is a sense of resignation and peace in the fact that if you are as low as you can possibly go, at least you can't go lower! There is a sense of "whatever comes, it's okay." This is an important principle. Part of the point of a trial is to build a humble, submissive character. In fact, that may be *the* point of the trial in your life: to elevate *God* and to lower *you!*

Fourth, *I am to acknowledge God's loving control*. God is not out to get you. He is not excited about how much pain you're experiencing. Heaven does not dance every time you cry out in agony. "For the LORD will not cast off forever, but, though he cause grief, he will have compassion according to the abundance of his steadfast love; for he does not afflict from his heart or grieve the children of men" (Lam 3:31-33). God is doing the afflicting, but it is for our good and for His glory!

God does not decree pain just for the sake of causing pain—that would be accusing God of sin. As Lamentations 3:34-36 reads, "To crush underfoot all the prisoners of the earth, to deny a man justice in the presence of the Most High, to subvert a man in his lawsuit, the LORD does not approve." But make no mistake, everything comes from Him. "Who has spoken and it came to pass, unless the LORD has commanded it? Is it not from the mouth of the Most High that good and bad come?" (Lam 3:37-38).

One commentator writes, "Instead of 'decreed' [commanded], we would say God 'permitted.'"[iii] This is an attempt to rescue God from the so-called "problem of evil" which asks the question, "How can evil co-exist with a God who is all-knowing, all-powerful, and all-good?" This word "command" is used 494 times in the Old Testament, and it *never* means to passively permit something. By far, it is translated most times as "command" but also includes "charge, appoint, order, instruct, give, commission, direct, ordain, and set in place." Notice the lack of passivity and the presence of proactivity. The "problem of evil" is only a problem from a human perspective. God doesn't look at evil and say, "Oh dear, what will I do about *that*?" However, we reach an intellectual wall where our ability to understand God stops with our current knowledge, so it requires that we wrestle with this issue.

Clearly, God is "of purer eyes than to see evil and cannot look at wrong" (Hab 1:13) and "God cannot be tempted with evil, and he himself tempts no one" (Jas 1:13). Yet God, in His infinitely holy and pure sovereignty, *uses the evil of human and angelic sin* to accomplish His perfect and glorious purposes. If this were *not* true, then by default all evil is outside the control of God and now the outcome of redemptive history is logically up for grabs. Instead, we see the horrible evil that happens in the world yet trust that God in using this for His overarching magnificent resolutions.

In an age when many in the church embrace a superficial faith, John Piper writes that "[the churches'] vision of God in relation to evil and suffering [is]…frivolous. The church has not been spending its energy to go deep with the unfathomable God of the Bible."[iv] One thing we know is this: God does not commit evil, but He ordains that it exists. The prophet Isaiah recorded, "I form light and create darkness, I make well-being and create calamity, I am the LORD, who does all these things" (Isa 45:7). Evil exists by God's permission and through the foreordained choice of those whom He created. Otherwise, we'd end up with a separate power that causes evil, in which case God would no longer be sovereign. However, evil is not a glitch in God's plan but rather an integral piece of God's plan!

In Luke 22:22 Jesus states, "For the Son of Man goes as it has been determined, but woe to that man by whom he is betrayed!" Jesus' betrayal was *God's* plan, even though the *betrayer* was responsible. Back in Lamentations 3, God achieves *His* purposes using what appears to be both good and bad things, but the end result of His will is always good. This is a "divine decree which uses and overrules the wicked acts of mankind to achieve God's purpose."[v] The Bible makes no apology about assigning the existence of calamity to God, yet God's holiness is never compromised.

God Made the River

Evil had come to Jerusalem. Jeremiah commented, "Why should a living man complain, a man, about the punishment of his sins?" (Lam 3:39). In this case the destruction had come as a result of sin, although that is not always the case. But this does bring us to an interesting point: punishment for sin is what is *due* to us!

And *this* is where Lamentations intersects so beautifully with the gospel! If you have come to saving faith in the Lord Jesus Christ, having repented of your sin and come humbly to Christ, not one tiny bit of your suffering is because of the judicial punishment for your sin. It may be for your sanctification and your loving discipline, but not for punishment. Christ is the one who bore the wrath of God against sin on your behalf.

So we begin our journey together in seeking Strength in the River. Jeremiah has given us our first lesson in walking through the river of tears. *God* made the river, *He* put you in the middle of it, and *you* are to trust Him because *He* knows what He is doing, for *great is His faithfulness!*

3

James Says,
"Solving the Problem is Not the Point"

A number of years ago, a young Christian mother gave an update about her family to fellow believers who were praying for her.[vi] She and her husband had just watched their three year-old-son die of leukemia. She wrote of her experience at the hospital—how she held her little boy as he looked up into Mommy's eyes for the last time, then relaxed and finally stopped breathing.

But wait! This isn't supposed to happen... especially not to *Christians*! But it does. And it's real. And we have to deal with it. What do we *do* when trials like this come to us?

James Understands

James 1:1-4 has much to say about suffering and trials. This passage is somewhat of a mystery and may even provoke strong emotion. James, the very first book of the New Testament to be written, stands alone among the epistles in jumping straight to exhortation.

The author is James, the half-brother of Jesus, natural child of Joseph and Mary. He was known as James the Just for his reputation of righteous behavior. James wrote to an unknown congregation of Jewish Christians, many of whom had been driven from their homes and possessions. They were being exploited by the rich, dragged into court, and slandered for their testimony as Christians, enduring sufferings of all kinds. He writes:

> James, a servant of God and of the Lord Jesus Christ, to the twelve tribes in the Dispersion: Greetings. Count it all joy, my brothers, when you meet trials of various kinds, for you know that the testing of your faith produces steadfastness. And let steadfastness have its full effect, that you may be perfect and complete, lacking in nothing (Jas 1:1-4).

At face value, James seems to be out of touch with reality. It appears that he doesn't understand the situation of suffering, but instead gives trite platitudes to just be happy no matter what. But James is no stranger to suffering.

James did not believe in Christ at first. Though Jesus was his half-brother, James was one of Jesus' family members who Mark 3:21 records as believing Jesus to be "out of his mind." But he did ultimately repent and worship his own brother. Likely, he watched as his friend and brother in Christ, Stephen, was stoned to death. He may have been among those in Acts 8:2, "[Some] devout men buried Stephen and made great lamentation over him." James saw the persecution of the new church in Jerusalem, which was scattered like dust in the wind. He *did*, in fact, understand suffering. He related warmly with his readers and wrote of "my brothers" more than eleven times.

Although James discusses many aspects of living the Christian life, he begins with joy in trials. The theme of the theology of suffering shows up in every chapter of James except chapter 3. He helps us view trials, tragedies, and tribulations in life as God-ordained circumstances that draw us to the arms of Jesus.

What is the Point?

James 1:1-4 is a great passage to *read*, but not an easy passage to *accept*. Let's be honest. Every one of us has difficulty accepting trials at times, and, in fact, verse 2 seems almost insensitive in the midst of heart-wrenching tragedies. "My health is failing; my spouse left me; I have broken relationships; I lost my job; my son has leukemia; my mother just died... and you're telling me to *consider it all joy*? Are you *kidding* me?! Don't you know how much this *hurts*?!"

At this rate, James 1:2 seems outright offensive and absolutely impossible. Your heart is so torn that you can't breathe, think, or pray. And when God feels ten million miles away, you cry out like Asaph did, "In the day of my trouble I seek the LORD; In the night my hand is stretched out without wearying; my soul refuses to be comforted... Has God forgotten to be gracious? Has he in anger shut up his compassion?" (Ps 77:2, 9). In other words, *"Where are you, God?"*

Jesus was perfectly sinless, yet He experienced deep sorrow here on earth. In John 13 Jesus grieved Judas' betrayal. He wept when He saw the grief of Mary and others over the death of her brother Lazarus. And at the thought of His own coming suffering, He was "very sorrowful, even to death" (Matt 26:38).

If we believe the goal of the Christian life is to be free of pain or to solve all our problems, then this passage doesn't make sense. We succumb to a false theology that says, "Struggling Christians are of a lesser order because they experience trials, while stronger Christians are blessed through a lack of trials." If this holds true, then James 1:2 is illogical, and we will skim over it uncomfortably.

James is asking us to wrestle with the paradox of *rejoicing* in affliction. We innately desire for our trials to have meaning and purpose, and to not be full of senseless pain. It begs the question, "Why?" This is the question we ask simply as an expression to God of our overwhelming sorrow.

For example, Jesus went through more suffering than any of us have or ever will. None of us will ever carry the weight of the sin of humanity. He alone completely understood the reason He was dying on a cross. He knew He was the Lamb of God, given for the sins of many, and He was in complete agreement with His Father's plan. And yet, at that ultimate moment of unspeakable physical, emotional, and spiritual agony, He said, "My God, my God, *why* have you forsaken me?" The point of James' message is that *solving the problem is not the point.* In a couple of pages, I will show you that instead of keeping the problem as the focus, the trials of life offer us three gifts: joy, endurance, and Christlikeness.

Before we get to the three gifts, we must have a foundation upon which to build. James 1 seems senseless without an understanding of the nature of God. We often don't walk in joy because we have a faulty view of God and His plan. We may think that God's plan revolves around *me* and that He exists for *my* sake. With this tiny view of God, trials don't make sense, and we feel unsafe. This may be basic information, but it is a necessary beginning. There are four cornerstones upon which we will build our joy, endurance, and Christlikeness.

Four Cornerstones

First, *God owns all things.* In Exodus 19:5 we learn that God owns everything and that "all the earth is mine." Job 41:11 says, "whatever is under the whole heaven is mine." Psalm 24:1 states, "The earth is the LORD's and the fullness thereof." There is no lack of clarity here; we are owned by our Maker.

Second, *God owns all things and causes all things.* Job said to his wife in Job 2:10, "Shall we receive good from God, and shall we not receive evil?" Jesus acknowledged exactly who was behind His impending death in John 6:38, "For I have come down from heaven, not to do my own will but the will of him who sent me." Yet Jesus never once got angry that His own Father was going to let Him die, or that His Father designed this plan from eternity past.

Yes, God causes all things in His all-encompassing sovereignty, but He uses secondary causes in accordance with His purity and holiness thus keeping Him above any wrong-doing whatsoever. It was God's plan for Jesus to die, yet those who crucified Him were sinners in need of forgiveness (Lu 23:34). God is sovereign as God, and men are responsible as moral beings. These two simultaneous truths exist together yet are unfath-omable to the mind of mere humans.

Third, *God owns all things, causes all things, and causes all things to work together for our good.* Romans 8:28 says, "And we know that for those who love God all things work together for good, for those who are called according to his purpose." Notice how it doesn't say just a few things, or some things, or most things, but *all* things! God truly desires good for you!

Fourth, *God owns all things, causes all things, causes all things to work together for our good, and causes all things to work together for His glory.* We are reminded by Romans 11:36, "For from him and through him and to him are all things. To him be glory forever. Amen."

If we don't understand this basic theological foundation of the nature of God, then we are robbed of joy in trials because we have an itsy-bitsy god who is unable to bear the weight of our pain. But when we understand that God owns all things, causes all things, causes all things to work together for our good, and causes all things to work together for His glory, *now our* God is big and we can trust Him with peaceful confi-dence! God never worries, has never been caught off-guard, has never had a committee meeting with angels to vote on what to do, and has never said, "Uh-oh" or "Oops." Ultimately, trials test how deeply we hold our conviction of an almighty, sovereign God. It's easy to *say* you believe in the sovereignty of God, but when a trial comes knocking on *your* door, do you really *believe* it?

The Gift of Joy

Now that we have a theological foundation, and solving the problem is not the point, we discover that in trials we receive the three gifts of joy, endurance, and Christlikeness. James tells his readers to "count it all joy" (Jas 1:2). What a strange way to address suffering saints! He doesn't begin with sympathy but jumps right to "be joyful." Why?

The difficulty with a trial is not what happens on the outside, but what happens on the inside; *that* is where the struggle lies—in the heart. To "count it all joy" means to form an opinion and make a conscious decision to think something. You must make a conscious choice to have a biblical view of your trial, which means you'll have to view it as *all* joy. Pure, complete, and refined joy.

These trials almost always hit us as a surprise. We don't schedule them… we *meet* them! The word "meet" means to fall into something or be surrounded by something—it's an unwelcome experience, a terrible surprise. In Luke 10 Jesus tells a parable of the Good Samaritan where "a certain man went down from Jerusalem to Jericho and fell among thieves." In Acts 27:40-41 Paul is shipwrecked and "they made for the beach. But striking [literally, *falling into*] a reef, they ran the vessel aground." These are accurate pictures of the nature of trials: being ambushed and running aground on a dangerous reef.

A trial is anything that puts us to the test. It can either be an external trial or an internal moral test, such as temptation. In this case James is speaking of outward tests. We've all heard it said that Christian joy has nothing to do with emotion. We can't say that our joy *depends* on our emotion, but don't buy for a minute that Christian joy is *devoid* of emotion!

Two phrases that occur dozens of times in the Psalms are "sing for joy" and "shout for joy." What greater and more noble purpose for our emotion can exist than to feel the joy of the Lord—to know that deep, abiding sense of peaceful confidence in God? And really, that's the synonym for joy… confidence in God!

Sometimes we assume we can only experience one emotion at a time, but Scripture shows us otherwise. The Apostle Paul described his own circumstances in 2 Corinthians 6:10 as "sorrowful, yet always rejoicing." David spoke of wonderful joy in Psalm 5:11, "But let all who take refuge in you rejoice; let them ever sing for joy, and spread your protection over them, that those who love your name may exult in you."

Where is this blessed joy found? Paul, likely facing execution while imprisoned in Rome for a second time, wrote to his beloved Timothy these words of encouragement in 2 Timothy 2:8, "Remember Jesus." Timothy was by now an accomplished pastor, a man of God that Paul called "my true child in the faith." Timothy knew Jesus, but Paul entreats him to *remember* Jesus. The intention wasn't to just recall something but to rehearse it, to be mindful of it. Or as the writer of Hebrews said, "looking to Jesus" (Heb 12:2). Remembering Jesus brings us the joy of which David writes.

Joy can't be based on the expectation that all your troubles will be solved. As much as we would like to put God in a neat little box where He allows a trial for a season and then gives total relief, this is not always the case. Yes, we *pray* for relief, but we *walk* in joy. We base our joy on the knowledge of God's character and His love for us. Our eyes are to be so focused on Christ that we can say with Job, "Though he slay me, I will hope in him" (Job 13:15). It's a joy that says, "Lord, it is Your will to bring this pain in my life, *so I trust You."*

Thankfully, in the midst of these trials, we have God's good promises to us. God assures us in Hebrews 13:5, "I will never leave you nor forsake you." Psalm 73:23, "I am continually with you; you hold my right hand."

Why name joy the *gift* in trials? Because trials keep us from becoming complacent about our loving God and Savior when we are forced to our knees and the tears won't stop. It is only then that our communion with our God is the purest. Trials drive us to run boldly to the throne of grace, to the safety of being on our faces in the presence of God, and to spend time in deep communion with God.

When we are hurting, we don't suffer as much from weak, shallow, and meaningless minutes with the Lord. We learn to relish and anticipate hours with God! The experience of communion and intimate fellowship with God is the very depiction of joy! It's the certainty that God owns all things, causes all things, causes all things to work together for our good, and causes all things to work together for His glory.

The Gift of Endurance

James 1:3 says, "for you know that the testing of your faith produces steadfastness." The word "produces" means "to accomplish, finish, or fashion something that is made." Trials test the reality and resolve of your faith. In 1 Peter 1:6-7 our trials are called the proof of our faith, and our response is to rejoice.

How a person handles trouble reveals the genuineness or lack of genuineness of his salvation experience. Does he have living faith or a dead faith that was never real? Does she cling all the more to Christ or reject Him in anger? James 1:12 says, "Blessed is the man who remains steadfast under trial, for when he has stood the test he will receive the crown of life, which God has promised to those who love him." "Stood the test" implies that you have proven your faith genuine, and that your trust in God hasn't been abandoned. Instead, it's been strengthened because your salvation has been shown to be genuine. This certainly doesn't mean that Christians do not falter in faith for a time; we are frail humans who don't always trust the Lord like we could. But the true believer ultimately always turns to Christ.

You can now look forward to the crown of life—eternity with God! This crown isn't given as a reward for enduring a trial, but the fact that you endured the trial has confirmed the genuineness of your salvation. What value can you put on the assurance of salvation? It is truly priceless. And our *trials* give us this gift!

A Refining Process

The testing of our faith is a refining process. In the same way a goldsmith uses fire to remove impurities foreign to the metal, God brings fire into your life to remove those sins which hurt most. God uses trials with a purpose in mind—He never wastes anything.

Here we get to the heart of the issue. Faith produces endurance, or steadfastness. "Steadfastness" implies staying behind or waiting patiently. This is not passive acceptance, but a persistent determination to walk through a trial as a winner, someone who clings tenaciously to God in perfect peace. This is patience that makes a man stand on his feet and face the storm head-on, being strong in the Lord. This is the active, heroic endurance to aggressively wait in the strength given by God. This is *exactly* what we need in trials and is promised to you as a believer in Christ. Steadfastness is a virtue gained gradually and painfully, not by reading books about perseverance, but by walking through pain.

As we walk through pain, God will refine our knowledge of Himself, His divine providence, and His holy purposes. Our *view* of God will get bigger and bigger, and our *faith* in God will grow in like manner. We know that God will always sustain and provide, even when all seems hopeless.

The presence of God is not just a theory to the suffering saint. God is the only reality we can count on.

Jesus Himself gave us a wonderful example of endurance in Hebrews 5:7, "In the days of his flesh, Jesus offered up prayers and supplications, with loud cries and tears, to him who was able to save him from death, and he was heard because of his reverence." Jesus knew exactly what was going to happen, all according to his Father's plan. So why was Jesus praying? Though fully and completely God, in His humanity, Jesus had a deep desire to pour out His heart and His emotion to His beloved Father. He needed to be in prayer to be in total communion and fellowship with God. This is endurance. This is perseverance. This is steadfastness.

We can receive the gift of endurance because of God's promises. "Draw near to God, and he will draw near to you" (Jas 4:8). God is the "God of all comfort" (2 Cor 1:3). "When the cares of my heart are many, your consolations cheer my soul" (Ps 94:19). "The LORD is my shepherd; I shall not want" (Ps 23:1). And now with endurance, we have a goal to accomplish: Christlikeness.

The Gift of Christlikeness

What happens when we allow our lives to be transformed by joy and endurance? "And let steadfastness have its full effect, that you may be perfect and complete, lacking in nothing" (Jas 1:4). The idea of "perfect" and "complete" refers to the process of adding virtue upon virtue until what you believe and how you act are the same.

Are you as faithful to God as He has been to you? No one can answer "yes." This reminds us of how gracious our God is to have saved us and brought us into eternal fellowship with Him. God is in the process of transforming you from an unfaithful man or woman to a faithful man or woman. This is the process of holiness and sanctification.

As far as our salvation is concerned, this is a finished work. Hebrews 10:14 states, "For by a single offering he has perfected for all time those who are being sanctified." On the other hand, as far as our current Christlikeness is concerned, we are a work in progress. Paul spoke of laboring on behalf of the Galatians until "Christ is formed in you" (Gal 4:19).

The strongest Christians are the ones carrying burdens. The faithful Christians, the ones who are walking in a manner worthy of the calling of Christ, walk as those who have gone through or are going through the purifying process of pain. Trials help us become more like Christ in so many ways. Here are just ten:

1. *Trials drive us to God's Word in new and desperate ways.* "It is good for me that I was afflicted, that I might learn your statutes" (Ps 119:71).

2. *Trials teach us deep, honest, real communion with God in prayer.* We can understand God in experiential reality. "As a deer pants for flowing streams, so pants my soul for you, O God" (Ps 42:1).

3. *Trials make us learn to walk in His power.* Paul asked the Lord to remove the thorn in his flesh, "Three times I pleaded with the Lord about this, that it should leave me. But he said to me, 'My grace is sufficient for you, for my power is made perfect in weakness.' Therefore I will boast all the more gladly of my weaknesses, so that the power of Christ may rest upon me" (2 Cor 12:8-9).

4. *Trials make us turn more and more to the Lord.* He may take away all other sources of comfort so that all we are left with is God. "In peace I will both lie down and sleep; for you alone, O LORD, make me dwell in safety" (Ps 4:8).

5. *Trials remind us that we are small and God is big.* Our focus and attention goes more and more to Him and less and less to ourselves. It makes us God-centered Christians instead of self-centered Christians. "Not to us, O LORD, not to us, but to your name give glory" (Ps 115:1).

6. *Trials give us genuine emotion of anticipation of our heavenly hope.* Paul enjoyed this emotion of anticipation. "For I consider that the sufferings of this present time are not worth comparing with the glory that is to be revealed to us" (Rom 8:18).

7. *Trials teach us to value God's blessings.* He gives us His care, His provision, our salvation, and many other gifts. "Rejoice in the LORD, O you righteous, and give thanks to his holy name!" (Ps 97:12).

8. *Trials make us more useful for Him.* We are more tenderhearted, less arrogant, more kingdom-focused, and more effective in service. Jesus told Peter, "Simon, Simon, behold, Satan has demanded to have you, that he might sift you like wheat, but I have prayed for you that your faith may not fail. And when you have turned again, strengthen your brothers" (Luke 22:31-32).

9. *Trials put God's mercy on display.* We showcase the grace of God when others see the joy-filled, peaceful confidence that someone undergoing trials displays! Speaking of God's coming mercy to Israel, the Lord "exalts himself to show mercy to you" (Isa 30:18).

10. *Trials shatter the idols of our own dreams and aspirations and make us live truly content with God's will.* "Only let your manner of life be worthy of the gospel of Christ" (Phil 1:27).

Ultimately, trials are a good thing in the life of a true believer. James is trying to tell us that solving the problem is *not* the point, but instead we need to receive the gifts of joy, endurance, and Christlikeness.

The young mother I mentioned at the beginning of the chapter wrote, on the day of her son's funeral, that this experience of saying goodbye to her beloved child was one she would treasure for the rest of her life. She spoke of death as being a moment she will *treasure*! Solving the problem was not the point of her trial. She walked in joy, endurance, and Christlikeness, and those blessings will strengthen her for the rest of her life.

God owns all things, causes all things, causes all things to work together for our good, and causes all things to work together for His glory. The Lord tenderly cares for you in the same way He cared for Lazarus by allowing him to die first, then by raising him from the dead. He weeps when you hurt, but He knows the good ending that He Himself has planned.

4

Jesus Says,
"Submit Willingly to the Plan of God"

The account of Jesus' birth in Luke 2:1-16 is an exciting, triumphant story of Jesus' entry into the world, full of promise and good news. But thirty years later, and about three and a half years into ministry, Jesus had made many enemies as well as disciples in Israel. Well aware that His arrest and crucifixion was the antithesis to the scene of His birth, Jesus walked toward His ultimate mission as the sacrificial Lamb of God.

> Then Jesus went with them to a place called Gethsemane, and he said to his disciples, "Sit here, while I go over there and pray." And taking with him Peter and the two sons of Zebedee, he began to be sorrowful and troubled. Then he said to them, "My soul is very sorrowful, even to death; remain here, and watch with me." And going a little farther he fell on his face and prayed, saying, "My Father, if it be possible, let this cup pass from me; nevertheless, not as I will, but as you will" (Matt 26:36-39).

Even in His perfect humanity, Jesus was filled with sorrow and grief at what was about to happen to Him. He knew that in just a matter of hours He would be nailed to a cross and would die a slow, cruel death in order to pay for the sins of humanity. He knew that He would bear the full weight of God's righteous fury and wrath against our unholiness and ungodliness.

Jesus, the righteous Son of God, both fully God and fully man, was now in the midst of a raging river of emotional anguish and growing anticipation of the unimaginable suffering that was before Him. What did He do in His time of deep suffering? He prayed a heartfelt and beautifully submissive prayer.

Submissively Accepting God's Plan

Many people ask, "What is God's plan for my life?" Thanks to Jeremiah, our understanding of the vastness of God's sovereignty has helped us know that God's plan is *whatever is happening right now*. God's plan can include something that you do not want to face or something that you will inevitably face. When you are diagnosed with an illness, short of the miraculous healing of the Lord, you *will* face the illness and the treatment. Many sick patients describe feeling trapped in their body, and they long to wake up from the nightmare just to feel "normal" again. Many people in counseling describe a longing for the difficult relationship to "just go away."

When you are in a difficult or even impossible relationship situation, the reality is that you will have to face it. But God's sovereignty is often bigger than we think, as proven in Isaiah 45:7, "I form light and create darkness, I make well-being and create calamity, I am the LORD, who does all these things."

This is precisely the situation in which Jesus finds Himself. He is faced with the culmination of the Father's plan for Him on earth—death by crucifixion—and He prays this simple prayer. Jesus was filled with sorrow and dread, yet He never sinned and never stopped trusting God even for one moment. The sinless Son of God is truly our best example of having strength in the river of suffering and our best example of being submissive to whatever God brings. How can we follow in His footsteps and peacefully accept the plan of God? We need to accept God's plan in resolution, prayer, trust, humility, and reverence.

Resolved Acceptance of God's Plan

First, accepting God's plan is done in resolution. It is a decision, a choice. It is a moment in time when you take a vote within yourself to please the Lord and say, "Yes, Lord, I accept whatever You bring."

Jesus resolved to accept God's plan. He brought His disciples to Gethsemane, a familiar place where they had been together many times. Gethsemane was a garden east of Jerusalem at the foot of the Mount of Olives. John's gospel calls it a "garden," but its name means "oil press." It was probably just an olive tree grove. The Greek term "place" is specific and could mean it was privately owned, implying that Jesus and His disciples had special permission to use the grove for teaching, fellowship and prayer.

In Matthew 26:39 Jesus went a little farther beyond His disciples. Luke's gospel tells us this was about a stone's throw away—close enough for the disciples to see and hear Him. This was an official moment. Jesus had partaken of His final Passover with the disciples, instituted the Lord's Table, offered encouragement and hope, and prayed earnestly for them in the great high priestly prayer of John 17. It was time to plead with the Lord that If there was any other way to accomplish the task of redemption, now would be a great time to jump in, because His arrest was only minutes away! But time was up and the Father was silent. Jesus laid down His will in surrender and submission, making an official resolution: "Not as I will, but as you will."

This is an important component of accepting God's plan: we don't just *resign* to God's will, we *affirm* God's will. We are given the option to accept or decline God's will with joy, just like any invitation. In a similar way, Job received an invitation from the Lord to walk through suffering. Job accepted, saying, "Shall we receive good from God, and shall we not receive evil?" (Job 2:10b). This wasn't a matter of choice to accept or decline the suffering (Job's ten children and all his earthly possessions were already taken away), but the choice he did have was how to receive it. The rest of the verse says, "In all this Job did not sin with his lips" (Job 2:10c).

If we have learned well the first two lessons, that God's sovereignty is bigger than you think and that solving the problem is not the point, then the clear response to suffering at any level is to simply tell the Lord, "I accept with full affirmation Your wisdom in doing as You see fit. I don't need answers. I don't need justification. I don't need some sort of explanation as to *why* this is happening; I just accept it." That is a type of faith that many Christians will never aspire to, but it's the resolution that produces peace and rest while the river rages around you.

Prayerful Acceptance of God's Plan

We also need to accept God's plan in prayer. Jesus went a little farther and prayed (Matt 26:39). This is probably the most obvious component of accepting God's plan, and yet it can be the most ignored. Certainly we pray, "God, get me out of this!" Perhaps instead we should pray, "God, do whatever You think is best."

A portion of one Puritan prayer asks for help in accepting God's plan:

> Help me, O Lord, to throw myself absolutely and wholly on Thee, for better, for worse, without comfort, and all but hopeless... grant that I may welcome Thy humbling in private so that I might enjoy Thee in public... Thou hast made me a monument of mercy, a trophy of redeeming power, in my distress let me not forget this.[vii]

In other words: "Let me receive what You are giving me here in the privacy of our time together so that I might exude the joy of the Lord when I am with others." This is *huge*! The writer accepts his trial on the basis that God has already saved him, and now his eternal salvation is a comfort and delight in the midst of temporary suffering.

When the river of suffering rages around you and you ignore prayer, there is no peace, righteousness, strength, growth, sustenance, joy, courage, and steadfastness. Paul wrote in his letter to the Philippians that the path to peace is prayer. This is one of the amazing benefits of suffering—you can fully expect to find your times of prayer with the Lord to be sweeter, more engaging, more passionate, and more focused. Don't expect to accept the plan of God without doing so in prayer. Make time to be specific in prayer. Give yourself the time, place, and solitude to bring your issue to the Lord, and to tell Him a thousand times if needed, "Whatever You decide is good with me!"

Trusting Acceptance of God's Plan

Jesus tenderly addresses God as "My Father" in His prayer, or as Mark's account records "Abba, Father," meaning "Daddy, Father." Right when it would seem that He was going to be abandoned to humiliation and death, Jesus knew His Father was near. Prayer was not a formal exercise of liturgically-inspired poetry, but instead an ongoing conversation about real issues deep within His heart. This was a safe place where He could quickly and easily walk into His Father's study at any time. He was never an interruption, never a bother, and was always given the full listening ear of His sympathetic Father. It was a place full of trust, hope, and confidence.

The Psalms are filled with prayers about trusting in the Lord. Psalm 13:5, "But I have trusted in your steadfast love." Psalm 28:7, "The LORD is my strength and my shield; in him my heart trusts, and I am helped; my heart exults, and with my song I give thanks to him." Psalm 31:14, "But I trust in you, O LORD; I say, 'You are my God.'"

Trust is not "I believe the Lord will get me out of this" or "I believe that God will prevail and this trial will lose." It is not "I believe that something really great will happen in my lifetime that will make all of this worthwhile" or "I believe God will show me why this is happening." Instead, trust is the belief that God knows precisely what He is doing, that you accept this, and that you will worship Him through it.

If going to the Lord is an uncomfortable experience for you because you seldom pray, then when you most need to run to your Father's arms for help, that same discomfort will still be there, and you will have even greater difficulty trusting the Lord for your trial. Cultivate your trust and familiarity with the Lord in prayer now so that when the hammer comes down, when the dam bursts, and when the earthquake hits, the door to the throne room of God is well-oiled and will open easily when you run through it!

Humble Acceptance of God's Plan

Jesus said, "If it be possible, let this cup pass from me" (Matt 26:39). In the Old Testament, the "cup" often alluded to suffering and the wrath of God. "Let him rain coals on the wicked; fire and sulfur and a scorching wind shall be the portion of their cup" (Ps 11:6). "Wake yourself, wake yourself, stand up, O Jerusalem, you who have drunk from the hand of the LORD the cup of his wrath, who have drunk to the dregs the bowl, the cup of staggering" (Isa 51:17).

In order to die, Jesus would have to endure suffering—not just physical suffering but also spiritual suffering as payment for our sin. About to face this unimaginable pain, Jesus was experiencing a very natural desire to shrink back from His task, so He asked His Father if perhaps there was another way that this pain could be avoided.

His prayer is offered with great respect and deference, making no demands of God. Jesus prays, "*If* it be possible." He doesn't claim deliverance from God, but instead makes a request in modest humility. In Mark 11:25 Jesus taught the proper attitude of prayer, "whenever you stand praying," but though the gospels record Jesus standing in prayer numerous times, this situation is intentionally different. In an attitude of reverence and surrender to His God and Father, Jesus fell on His face to pray. He clearly wasn't pressing for anything outside His Father's will. This wasn't a question of whether or not He should do what was asked; it was a question of whether or not the cross was the *only* way to God's will.

How often do we go to the Lord begging and demanding answers before stopping to do so in humility and deference? There is tremendous joy and peace in humbling yourself before the Lord. He is glorified and you are not, and it is the proper position for both of you! Perhaps another benefit of your trial is that it has reminded you to fall on your face before the Holy God. Humility is the only spiritual posture of accepting God's plan that gives you the opportunity to feel completely safe in your hour of need.

Reverent Acceptance of God's Plan

Jesus concluded, "Nevertheless, not as I will, but as You will." The final petition of His prayer is that the Father would accomplish His own will. This is the pattern of Jesus' entire life, "I do nothing on my own authority, but speak just as the Father taught me" (John 8:28b). As both God and man, Jesus willingly subjugated Himself to the will of His Father.

Notice the unconditional submission. Jesus has already tenderly approached the Father, asking if there might be another way. However, He knows that there is something bigger and more important than His own desire: the will of His Father. The opportunity to redeem God's people far outweighs the fear of His own suffering and death.

This is a whole new level of reverence to the Lord! We might sincerely pray, "Lord, not what I will but what You will," but how often is this really just code language for, "Oh, please do it my way, but if You have to do it Your way then I guess I'll deal with it," as if God's will, though painful, is not the best option?

To accept God's plan in reverence means that your number one priority is for God to be glorified. His plan needs to be carried out, even if this plan includes you standing in a raging river of suffering. Reverence says, "God, I not only accept Your will, but I pray deeply and earnestly that Your will is carried out. Your will is always best, and if this river is Your will, then please give me the grace to rejoice in it."

Jesus was able to accept God's plan in resolution, in prayer, in trust, in humility, and in reverence. This doesn't mean that Jesus didn't experience any feelings of emotional agony. He still needed strength to face what was coming, and His "soul [was] very sorrowful, even to death" (Mark 14:34). Looking closely, we find that there are actually two parallel tracks happening at the same time—Jesus' personal anguish and His perfect acceptance of God's plan.

Fellowshipping in Christ

When Jesus and His disciples finished the Passover, Jesus didn't look at His watch and say, "Well, guys, time's up. I'm headed to Gethsemane to pray. See you after the resurrection." Luke's gospel tells us that Jesus went,

"As was his custom, to the Mount of Olives, and the disciples followed him" (Luke 22:39). He was going to a familiar place with familiar people. Judas had been dismissed and was setting up the betrayal, but the faithful eleven walked with Jesus.

Jesus wanted His disciples to stay close, and although He had to face this moment with the Lord alone, He would "go over there" just within eyesight. In His humanity, Jesus needed the support and fellowship of His best friends on this earth. Those who would arrest Jesus were coming soon, and He needed watchers, those who could support Him with their love and care while He prayed.

Not only did Jesus bring His close group of friends with Him, but He also narrowed it down even more to just His three closest men: Peter, James, and John. He was free to be open and vulnerable and wasn't afraid to let His emotions show. He let the full weight of His suffering sweep over Him, and even told His friends how He was feeling and that He *needed* them. Jesus availed Himself of the fellowship of His closest friends in His hour of need, which, by the way, helps explain His great disappointment when He found them asleep.

When we say the word "fellowship" in the American church, the first things that usually come to mind are food and gathering. The fellowship of the saints, however, is infinitely deeper than just enjoying smiles and hugs as we get to know one another in Christ. It's perhaps best condensed by the phrase Paul used in Romans 12:15 to "Rejoice with those who rejoice, weep with those who weep."

This is why you cannot be a loner in the body of Christ. When *your* time of need comes, you will need the relationships you have sought out and formed. Join a Small Group at your church, go to Sunday School, and rotate sitting with four different people. Get involved in ministry. When you see someone in need, be that person to reach out and pray. Put yourself out there and take the initiative to form relationships. Don't wait for a church program to facilitate it for you. The church does its best, but ultimately it's the individual believers in deep relationships that make godly fellowship happen.

Weeping in Christ

Hebrews 5:7 states that, "In the days of his flesh, Jesus offered up prayers and supplications, with loud cries and tears, to him who was able to save him from death, and he was heard because of his reverence." The phrase "loud cries" is translated literally as "powerful and mighty," "wailing," "shouting," and "clamor" as to the depths of one's soul. Luke's gospel tells us that Jesus was perspiring in prayer and that His "sweat became like great drops of blood falling down to the ground." This is most likely a rare condition called *hematidrosis*, which is caused by extreme mental and emotional strain in which capillaries in the skin dilate and burst, releasing blood.

Accepting God's plan is not a static, emotionless event. Emotion as a result of tragedy is not sin; rejecting God's sovereignty and responding in anger or impatience is sin. Yes, we accept God's plan in humble submission, but this doesn't mean we don't go before Him to weep and wail.

Many believers get spiritually stuck in the midst of trials because they haven't laid it all down in the Lord's presence. When you pray, lay your sin at the feet of the Lord. We pray little anemic prayers for help, but we don't often take the time to get alone and pray with determination, "Okay, I'm not getting off my face until I have nothing left mentally, physically, or emotionally. I'm going to cry out to God like I never have before."

Persisting in Christ

Jesus already knew the plan the Father had set for Him. He knew that Psalm 22 was a prophetic description of the crucifixion of the suffering Servant of God. He knew that the prophetic words of David, "My God, my God, why have you forsaken me?" were ultimately penned for Him. He knew that His bones would be out of joint, that "they have pierced my hands and feet" and that "they divide my garments among them and for my clothing they cast lots" was speaking of Him and His clothing (Ps 22:16, 18).

Jesus knew that the suffering Servant in Isaiah 53 referred to Himself. He would be pierced for our transgressions, crushed for our iniquities, and the Lord would lay on Him the iniquity of us all. He would be oppressed and afflicted, a Lamb led to slaughter. He would die, and His grave would be with the wicked. Jesus even knew that as Isaiah said, "it was *the will of the Lord* to crush him" (Isa 53:10, emphasis added).

Yet, Jesus was persistent to ask in prayer. He kept asking over and over again, even though (unlike us in our situations) He already knew the plan. Not only did He return three times to pray, but both Mark 14:35 and Luke 22:41 state that "He prayed." In both instances, this is an imperfect verb meaning, "He kept on praying." We have only a small synopsis of Jesus' prayers from that night, but He must have prayed for a long time. He prayed long enough for the disciples to all fall asleep, so He wasn't gone for just a few minutes.

What was He praying? What took Him so long? We know that pure repetition isn't the key to having God answer your prayers. In Matthew 6:7–8 Jesus taught, "And when you pray, do not heap up empty phrases as the Gentiles do, for they think that they will be heard for their many words. Do not be like them, for your Father knows what you need before you ask him." So what was Jesus doing? He knew that God's answer wasn't going to change!

Jesus was affirming His agreement with the will of the Father. For us as sinful men and women, prayer is not designed to align God with our will, but to align our will with God. Prayer is not to make God more like *us* but to make us more like *God*. It should firm up the muscles of our faith.

Jesus was building spiritual muscle—spiritual resolve. He persisted in prayer and sought much-needed encouragement and fellowship with His sleeping disciples, persisted in prayer again, then hoped again for the comfort of His friends, and went back to prayer one more agonizing time to be fully strengthened for the torment that lay ahead. God would give Him strength for the ordeal, and He would also give Him strength to persist in prayer. At some point in His prayer time, Luke's gospel tells us that, "there appeared to him an angel from heaven, strengthening him. And being in agony he prayed more earnestly" (Luke 22:43-44). The Greek word "earnestly" means "continuously, zealously, fervently, mightily" and comes from a verb that means "to be stretched out."

Jesus submitted willingly to the plan of God while fellowshipping, weeping, and persisting. As a result, He emerged ready for battle with strength and resolve to face His hour of trial with courage. Heaven listened and sent help!

When Jesus finished praying, He returned to His disciples a third time. With strength of conviction He said, "Rise, let us be going; see, My betrayer is at hand." Just then Judas arrived with a crowd, carrying swords, clubs, lanterns, and torches. But Jesus took the initiative. John 18:4–5, "Then Jesus, knowing all that would happen to him, came forward and said to them, 'Whom do you seek?' They answered him, 'Jesus of Nazareth.' Jesus said to them, 'I am he.'" All the soldiers fell to the ground as the Great I AM spoke with authority, revealing His identity. Then Jesus asked them again, "Whom do you seek?" In the midst of six different trials, He exhibited courage and strength, through floggings, beatings, and a crown of thorns. He was mostly silent, but when He did speak it was with strength and authority.

All four gospels are surprisingly brief and to the point about the crucifixion of Christ. All four simply say, "They crucified him." Jesus endured the wrath of God on the cross, and when the debt had been paid He declared, "It is finished." When all that was left to do was to actually die (unlike the typical death of a crucified victim, in which breathing becomes impossible) Luke's gospel tells us, "Jesus, calling out with a loud voice, said, 'Father, into your hands I commit my spirit.'" Matthew says, "Jesus cried out with a loud voice and yielded up his spirit." Mark says, "Jesus uttered a loud cry and breathed his last." Jesus took a deep breath, cried out in victory, and died *on purpose*.

How was He able to do this? He submitted willingly and powerfully to the plan of God. When you, too, are standing in the torrent of the river of suffering, submit and receive the power to endure, and the same strength given to Christ will be yours as well.

5

Abraham Says,
"Trust in the Integrity of God"

As Christians, the often-used phrase "trust the Lord" can almost become part of our "Christianese" language, but what do we *really* mean by this phrase? That we really just want God to do whatever we want? Or that we can pray in a certain magical way so He fulfills our will? Certainly God answers prayers, and He does things we ask of Him all the time. In His sovereign purpose He causes all things, and one of the means by which He accomplishes His will is through our prayers. But sometimes we let this wonderful provision from the Lord lead us to a shallow view of what it means to trust God.

We want to be strong in our faith and have a biblical understanding of a proper response to the trials that the Lord brings. *This* is what it means to really *trust* God! It means completely believing His integrity. He is the "only wise God [to whom] be glory forevermore" (Rom 16:27). "With God are wisdom and might; he has counsel and understanding" (Job 12:13), and as Jesus said, "My sheep hear my voice, and I know them, and they follow me. I give them eternal life, and they will never perish… my Father, who has given them to me, is greater than all, and no one is able to snatch them out of the Father's hand" (John 10:27-29).

To trust the integrity of God means to look beyond the moment and into eternity at just how wise God will show Himself to be. In what is arguably the single greatest instance of trusting the integrity of God by anyone other than Christ, we want to examine the most difficult test God ever gave: when Abraham was commanded to sacrifice his son Isaac.

God's Promises to Abraham

Abraham's life of following after God commenced when he left Ur of the Chaldees. God promised Abram (before his name was changed to Abraham) in Genesis 12 that he would be made into a great nation, that he would be blessed, and that all the nations of the earth would be blessed in him.

Over many years this promise was repeated in various ways to Abram. The Lord first appeared to him when he had just recently entered Canaan. It was then that God promised the land of Canaan to Abram's offspring. Later, in Genesis 13, God took Abram to Ramoth Nazor (the highest point in central Israel) to look all around. God told him that everything he could see would belong to his offspring forever, and that his offspring would be as numerous as the dust of the earth.

Some time had passed, and after Abram rescued his nephew Lot from the kings of the north, he started fretting one night over the fact that God had made all these promises to him, yet he still didn't have a son. God showed Abram the stars in the sky and promised that his offspring would be as numerous as the stars. Genesis 15:6 recounted that "He believed the LORD, and he counted it to him as righteousness."

The next day Abram obeyed God's instructions to arrange the parts of slain sacrificial animals in two columns, representing two parties that were making a covenant together. God would pass between the pieces, in essence saying, "May I become like these animals if I do not fulfill my part of the covenant." He wanted to make sure Abram understood that from his own body would come a people, and that the land of Canaan would belong to these people.

Since this was an unconditional covenant, God made Abram fall asleep so that God alone was responsible for the covenant. When the sun had set, God appeared as a flaming furnace in the darkness and passed solemnly through the slain animals. God alone would keep this covenant, and Abram would enjoy the benefits of God's unconditional promises.

Years later, when Abram was ninety-nine years old and God was preparing him for the covenant of circumcision, God changed Abram's name to Abraham, which means "Father of many." God was showing Abraham that he would be fruitful and that a chosen nation with kings would come from his descendants. Then God also renamed Abraham's wife from Sarai to Sarah, meaning "Princess," because she would have the son from whom kings would come and from whom the ultimate King of kings would someday come. Lastly, God named their unborn son Isaac, meaning "laughter." Sarah laughed at this promise, but "Little Laughter" was on his way!

Throughout all these years, Abraham's faith had been unsteady at times, like ours. He had lied to Pharaoh and Abimelech about Sarah not being his wife, and he had tried to make God's promise happen sooner by having a child with Hagar. This only made matters worse and started sixteen years of misery in the home until Hagar and her son Ishmael finally departed.

"Little Laughter," Isaac, was born when Abraham was 100 years old. This was nearly twenty-five years after the first promise that God had made! But Abraham and Sarah, the "Father of many" and "Princess" finally held "Laughter" in their arms. Genesis 21:6–7 says, "And Sarah said, 'God has made laughter for me; everyone who hears will laugh over me.' And she said, 'Who would have said to Abraham that Sarah would nurse children? Yet I have borne him a son in his old age.'"

Isaac grew and enjoyed the love of his parents. They watched him grow from a baby to a toddler to a young boy to a young man, but when Isaac was a teenager the Lord called to Abraham and destroyed his whole world in one crushing command.

Look Beyond Your Emotion

To trust in God means to look beyond the immediate and into the infinite. There are at least six points on the horizon that we need to look beyond: our emotion, our opinion, our selfishness, our choices, our pride, and our lifetime. First, let's look beyond our emotion.

Genesis 22:1-2 begins, "After these things God tested Abraham and said to him, 'Abraham!' And he said, 'Here I am.' He said, 'Take your son, your only son Isaac, whom you love, and go to the land of Moriah, and offer him there as a burnt offering on one of the mountains of which I shall tell you.'" Although the author reassures us that God was merely testing Abraham, *Abraham* did not know at the time that this was a test. He was about to be stretched and tested, but his faith was also about to grow.

The emotionally endearing terms God used must have been agonizing for Abraham to hear, "Your *son*... your *only* son... your only son *Isaac*... your only son Isaac whose name means *Laughter*... your only son Isaac whom you *love*." Isaac was a teenager by now and had been Abraham's laughter and joy for fifteen years or so, but now all laughter was gone. Laughter would have to die. The Lord commanded Abraham to worship Him in a way that would test his faith and trust in God. This worship would be accomplished with a burnt offering of his only son.

The text says "burnt offering" in a simple, sanitized way, but a burnt offering meant more than just that. A burnt offering involved cutting the offering's throat, dismembering it, and burning its body parts on an altar until all that remained were ashes.

Human sacrifice was a common cultural practice in Abraham's day. Abraham was familiar with this practice because it had taken place in Ur and was also part of the Canaanite culture. Human sacrifice was part of Abraham's worldview, despite how horrifying and repulsive it was to the Lord. He didn't have the written Law of God to inform him about the doctrine of God, and yet not for one moment did Abraham doubt or question the Lord.

How did Abraham feel about sacrificing his only son? The text doesn't tell us, but we can only guess his devastation, shock, and confusion. He was reminded in a single instant that he was small and God was big. He must have understood at that point that to be a worshiper of God is no insignificant thing. And yet the text makes no mention of Abraham's response, thoughts, or emotions he must have had at the astonishment of such a command.

When you walk through a river of agony or trial, your emotions usually kick into high gear. Depending on the situation, you might experience grief, anger, frustration, indignation, sadness, depression, confusion, hopelessness, or despair. If we let our emotions dictate our response, then we have said to the river, "I'm going to lie on my back and let you sweep me away."

In fact, dealing with how you *feel* about the situation can become the major focus of trying to get through it. We can be in a desperate quest to feel better, and we sin by trying to numb the pain with substances or food or entertainment instead of responding biblically to the situation itself.

Regarding Abraham's emotions, the text is neutral. The text doesn't say that he either ignored or was consumed by them, so the conspicuous omission of Abraham's emotions tells us that he must have looked beyond them. He simply stepped forward one step at a time to obey the Lord.

We acknowledge that emotion is a major component of suffering. Paul commanded us in Romans 12:15 to "weep with those who weep," but part of trusting the integrity of God is realizing that the emotion does not have to control you or your response. God will turn weeping into rejoicing—maybe sooner or maybe later, but He will—and each day you will take one step closer to that day.

Look Beyond Your Opinion

Like a precious child, Abraham obeyed God immediately, without question.

So Abraham rose early in the morning, saddled his donkey, and took two of his young men with him, and his son Isaac. And he cut the wood for the burnt offering and arose and went to the place of which God had told him. On the third day Abraham lifted up his eyes and saw the place from afar (Gen 22:3-4).

Abraham took two servants along with Isaac. They would most likely have been young men about Isaac's age, since the word "boy" in verse 5 referring to Isaac is the same word as "young men" in verse 3 referring to the servants. They must have cut a lot of wood, which was why they needed a donkey to carry it as well as their provisions.

It was a three-day journey by foot to Mt. Moriah from the land of the Philistines where Abraham had been living as a nomad (21:34). God was directing them to a specific place, and Abraham had three agonizing days to contemplate what he was about to do.

> Then Abraham said to his young men, "Stay here with the donkey; I and the boy will go over there and worship and come again to you." And Abraham took the wood of the burnt offering and laid it on Isaac his son. And he took in his hand the fire and the knife. So they went both of them together (Gen 22:5-6).

The ascent up Mt. Moriah became too steep for the donkey, so Abraham laid the huge woodpile on top of Isaac's strong shoulders and they went up together, just father and son. Abraham obeyed the Lord down to the last detail, fully intending to sacrifice Isaac exactly as he was told. Again, he didn't express his own opinion on the matter, but received the word of the Lord and promptly obeyed.

You might think, "Well, good for him, I would have done the same thing!" Not necessarily! Wait until a life situation happens, in which Scripture calls *you* to do the very last thing you want to do... like be patient or forgive or abide by the law of Christ as expressed in the New Testament.

We don't get to decide which parts of the Word of God are worth obeying—our *opinions* are irrelevant. Scripture tells us how to handle times of prosperity and blessing and times of great agony and pain, "Only let your manner of life be worthy of the gospel of Christ" (Phil 1:27). Your opinion as to whether or not this trial should be happening to you is not the issue. You have to look beyond that.

When obedience to Christ involves suffering, we should disregard our personal feelings. We can't go looking for loopholes or ways to get out of obedience on a technicality. Just because we don't like a situation, it doesn't give us the right to play the victim and decide we need to make our own rules about it. Either Christ *is* our Lord or He is *not*. Trusting the integrity of God means knowing that God knows what He's doing, and knowing that He doesn't require our opinion on the matter.

Look Beyond Your Selfishness

Everything was going according to plan. Then Isaac spoke up and asked an innocent question, which must have pained Abraham to the core. "And Isaac said to his father Abraham, 'My father!' And he said, 'Here I am, my son.' He said, 'Behold, the fire and the wood, but where is the lamb for a burnt offering?'" (Gen 22:7).

What a heart-breaking question! Isaac's question showed that he didn't have the full picture yet but still completely trusted his beloved father. Abraham gave a truthful answer, leaving open the possibility of God providing an alternate way to obey Him. "Abraham said, 'God will provide for himself the lamb for a burnt offering, my son'" (22:8).

This was a statement of truth, regardless of whether or not Isaac was the sacrifice, and it was said in a way to comfort and deflect fear from a naïve Isaac. Abraham was no doubt emotionally distraught, focused on what must have been intense suffering that we can't fully understand, and yet he took the time and effort to tenderly shepherd Isaac. Abraham walked with Isaac every step of the way. He assured Isaac of God's love and his own love.

Abraham could have been selfish, thinking only about how this trial was affecting himself, but instead he considered Isaac. He didn't burden his son with what he didn't need to know but took this last opportunity to give comfort and care. Abraham wasn't relieved of his responsibility to love those closest to him—he wasn't supposed to stop being a positive role model of trust in the Lord. By now Isaac was probably sensing that something was up, but Abraham told him the thing he most needed to hear: "God will provide."

Suffering can often be an excuse for us to surrender our responsibility to think of others as more important than ourselves. Men, when you or someone in your family is suffering, it is your responsibility to shepherd your wife and your family through this. You need to assure them of God's care and of your own love for them.

When you are the one facing a trial, you have a responsibility to assure those around you that you trust the Lord. You need to set an example of walking through the river with an honest, heart-felt belief in the integrity of God and demonstrate patience and dignity, even as the Lord lets the waters rise.

Look Beyond Your Choices

"When they came to the place of which God had told him, Abraham built the altar there and laid the wood in order and bound Isaac his son and laid him on the altar, on top of the wood" (Gen 22:9).

Abraham couldn't have offered Isaac without his son's cooperation. At some point during verse 9, Abraham told Isaac what must happen. It is likely that Abraham was at least 115 years old and Isaac at least 15, and yet Isaac obeyed his father and willingly allowed himself to be bound and put on the altar. He most likely climbed up onto the altar and allowed himself to be bound to prevent a last-second fearful fleeing away. Many parents have had to face the agony of seeing a child die, but the agony of being the *instrument* of that death must have been unimaginable.

Then came one of the most dramatic moments in all of the Bible, "Then Abraham reached out his hand and took the knife to slaughter his son" (22:10). Abraham had plenty of chances to back out of his responsibility, and this was the final moment to decide between obedience and faintheartedness. He didn't look around for an alternative, didn't hesitate, and didn't beg God to relent. He knew that no sacrifice was too hard when his loving God required it of him.

So he reached for his blade to cut Isaac's throat. He braced himself to hold Isaac's head back as he prepared to cut hard through his neck as quickly as possible. By now there was no doubt that Abraham trusted God with genuine faith, for this was the ultimate test. True faith produces obedience, and obedience proves that faith is valid. James spoke of this exact instance in James 2:21-22, "Was not Abraham our father justified by works when he offered up his son Isaac on the altar? You see that faith was active along with his works, and faith was completed by his works."

Abraham wanted to be a man of faith, but he knew two things: first, that Isaac was the child of promise around whom the entire future of God's chosen nation was planned, and second, that God wanted Abraham to sacrifice Isaac. Even though he couldn't understand how they fit together, he believed that God could reconcile these two truths.

Abraham looked beyond the choices that were presented to him, trusting that God would turn this impossible situation into something good. Somehow, he knew that God would work it all out, because in verse 5 Abraham had said, "We're going to worship, and we will *both* come back when we're done." Thanks to inspired revelation of the New Testament, we also find out that:

> By faith Abraham, when he was tested, offered up Isaac, and he who had received the promises was in the act of offering up his only son, of whom it was said, "Through Isaac shall your offspring be named." He considered that God was able even to raise him from the dead (Heb 11:17-19).

Abraham so completely believed God's promise that Isaac would carry on the promised nation of God that he figured the only possible way was that God would raise Isaac from the dead, from the ashes of the burnt offering. It's important to remember that Abraham had a very basic, limited understanding of God. With less knowledge of God than a typical first grade Sunday School child, Abraham hardly knew about resurrection from the dead, yet he based his trust in God's integrity and in God's command to sacrifice Isaac. Abraham figured that God would do something miraculous—and He did.

Often, it's our fear of the unknown that causes us to sin and not trust the Lord in the midst of trials. We fear that if we obey the Lord, it's going to hurt too much and we can't handle that. This is why people are tempted to leave difficult marriages. They think, "If I stay it might hurt, and I just can't picture things getting any better." But if you're Abraham you'd say, "I *know* things aren't going to get better—my *son* is going to *die*—but I need to look beyond the limited choices and options I have and choose to believe that the Lord just might surprise me with His faithfulness!"

Look Beyond Your Pride

Abraham trusted God and was not surprised at the idea that God could raise Isaac from a pile of ashes, but he *was* surprised when "the angel of the LORD called to him from heaven and said, 'Abraham, Abraham!' And he said, 'Here I am'" (Gen 22:11).

Verse 11 parallels verse 1, but with greater intensity. In the Old Testament, specific references to "the angel of the Lord" refer to the Son of God. Abraham was thrilled to hear the voice of the Lord speaking directly to him. Isaac was probably pretty happy about it, too! Abraham was told the purpose of his trial when the Son of God replied in Genesis 22:12, "He said, 'Do not lay your hand on the boy or do anything to him, for now I know that you fear God, seeing you have not withheld your son, your only son, from me.'" The heart of the test was to reveal the truth that Abraham feared God.

One author writes, "The true worshiper fears the Lord; that is, the true worshiper draws near to the Lord in love and adoration and reverence but shrinks back in fear of such an awesome deity."[viii] The one who fears the Lord understands that no matter the cost, complying with the Word of God is his or her main responsibility. God is all-knowing; He wasn't trying to find out if Abraham really feared Him or not. The test was for Abraham's sake—to stretch him to the furthest limits of demonstrating that his faith was authentic.

What if certain trials are brought into your life just to test your willingness to obey the Lord through them? What if that is the *primary* reason for the trial? What if you are given trials to stretch you and make you more obedient, to make you stop fighting for your so-called "rights"? Remember, you are a purchased slave of Jesus Christ, and your rights, your property, and your dreams belong to Him—and ultimately are *found* in Him! This results in "praise and glory and honor at the revelation of

Jesus Christ" (1 Pet 1:7). A wonderful result of walking through the river of tears is that Psalm 115:1 takes on a whole new meaning, "Not to us, O LORD, not to us, but to your name give glory, for the sake of your steadfast love and your faithfulness!"

Even in the midst of a test, God was gracious and merciful, "And Abraham lifted up his eyes and looked, and behold, behind him was a ram, caught in a thicket by his horns. And Abraham went and took the ram and offered it up as a burnt offering instead of his son" (Gen 22:13). Behind the scenes—literally, behind Abraham—the Lord was already providing a way of deliverance: a sacrificial ram as a substitute for Isaac. "So Abraham called the name of that place, 'The LORD will provide'; as it is said to this day, 'On the mount of the LORD it shall be provided'" (Gen 22:14). The God who tests is also the God who provides for you.

Look Beyond Your Lifetime

> And the angel of the LORD called to Abraham a second time from heaven and said, "By myself I have sworn," declares the LORD, "because you have done this and have not withheld your son, your only son, I will surely bless you, and I will surely multiply your offspring as the stars of heaven and as the sand that is on the seashore. And your offspring shall possess the gate of his enemies, and in your offspring shall all the nations of the earth be blessed, because you have obeyed my voice" (Gen 22:15–18).

God reiterated the unconditional promises He had already made to Abraham, but the reiteration was only given *after* the testing of Abraham's faith. Other than Christ on the cross, this is perhaps the most awe-inspiring test of faith in Scripture! This test brought him to the brink of human emotion and thought; he had to surrender all his hopes and dreams that revolved around this one boy. He demonstrated the heart of real worship: to fear God no matter what the cost. This is the belief that the Lord will provide. You can suffer and sacrifice without reservation and without hesitation.

For the first time in the Bible, God swears an oath by His own name. Hebrews 6:13-15 tells us that, "For when God made a promise to Abraham, since he had no one greater by whom to swear, he swore by himself, saying, 'Surely I will bless you and multiply you.' And thus Abraham, having patiently waited, obtained the promise." God wanted Abraham to look beyond his lifetime to the good that God promised would come true. He *always* keeps His word. God is a God of integrity.

One of the joys of trials is that they encourage you to think beyond your short lifetime, to stop idolizing the perfect life or seeing yourself as above certain circumstances. This means taking the long view to stop believing that you have to pursue your own personal happiness in your lifetime. The irony is that if you do this successfully, you actually do get your own personal happiness in this lifetime, because it doesn't matter what your circumstances are—you choose your attitude!

Look carefully, and you'll notice shadows of the cross, stamped like a watermark behind Abraham's story. This almost-sacrifice of Isaac took place on Mt. Moriah. It's no coincidence that 2 Chronicles 3 notes that this would be the site of Solomon's temple—the official site of sacrifice and worship for the Jew. It was here that Jesus would proclaim the kingdom and be rejected. Just as Isaac carried his own sacrificial wood to the place of sacrifice, Jesus would be whipped and beaten and given His own wooden cross to carry to Golgotha.

What does it mean to really trust God? It means to completely trust His integrity, that He is the "only wise God [to whom] be glory forevermore" (Rom 16:27), that "with God are wisdom and might; he has counsel and understanding" (Job 12:13), that as Jesus said, "[True believers] hear my voice, and I know them, and they follow me… and no one is able to snatch them out of the Father's hand" (John 10:27, 29). To trust the integrity of God means to look beyond the moment into eternity at just how wise God will show Himself to be.

6

Ruth Says,
"Let Your Godly Character
Shine Through"

Several centuries after the conquest of Canaan by the Israelite people, memories of triumphant victories under Joshua had been replaced by spiritual inconsistency and decline. During this dark time in Israel's history, the apostasy of Israel escalated into a massive corruption of civil war and chaos in Israel. They had no king and had turned away from the Lord at least six different times.

Judges 21:25 reports, "In those days there was no king in Israel. Everyone did what was right in his own eyes." Israel was characterized by spiritual weakness, void of moral character. There were few people left who truly worshiped the Lord with an internal reality of faith or a desire to obey His Word. Even one of the great heroes of the time, Gideon, by whose hand the invading Midianites were defeated, eventually failed to seek the Lord. He broke God's law in regard to his family, ending in a bloodbath for almost all of his seventy sons.

But against the blackness of spiritual darkness and difficulty, we find a beautiful diamond shining forth in the midst of tragedy. We read an amazing story of faith in the Lord—a love story between a woman and her God, her family, and her husband. This woman was, of course, Ruth.

The Story of Ruth

The story begins with Elimelech, his wife Naomi, and their two adult sons, Mahlon and Chilion. Famine in Israel drove this Jewish family from Bethlehem to Moab, about fifty miles east on the other side of the Dead Sea. The Moabites were genetically related to Israel through Lot, but were excluded as a people from the congregation of the Lord. Shortly after arriving in Moab, Elimelech died, after which Mahlon and Chilion took Moabite wives—Orpah and Ruth. They stayed in Moab another ten years, and through events not explained in Scripture both Mahlon and Chilion died.

Naomi was left without a provider and without sons to care for her. She decided it was time to go home to Israel and told her two Moabite daughters-in-law, Orpah and Ruth, to go back to their parents to find new husbands. At first both of them said, "No! We will go with you!" Orpah changed her mind, but Ruth said, "Do not urge me to leave you or to return from following you. For where you go I will go, and where you lodge I will lodge. Your people shall be my people, and your God my God" (Ruth 1:16). Naomi and Ruth returned to Bethlehem during the barley harvest around March or April. Naomi, gone for over a decade and somewhat unrecognizable, stirred up the whole town, and the women whispered among themselves, "Is this Naomi?"

Chapter 2 begins, "Now Naomi had a relative of her husband's, a worthy man of the clan of Elimelech, whose name was Boaz." Boaz was certainly older than Ruth, but he was also "worthy." In Hebrew this is two words that meant he was a strong, self-assured man of character. Significantly, Boaz was the *opposite* of what most of Israel had become during the time of the judges. He was a true worshiper of the Lord, well-respected and admired.

Ruth wanted to serve her mother-in-law, so she offered to collect grain for bread. According to the Law of Moses, the poor were allowed to glean in the fields, gathering what the workers had dropped or missed.

Ruth found a field and began collecting grain, learning quickly that the owner of the field, Boaz, was a kind man. When Ruth came home after a long day of hard work, Naomi asked in whose field she had worked. When she answered, "Boaz," Naomi was overjoyed, explaining that the man was a close relative of theirs—a kinsman-redeemer.

A kinsman-redeemer was a family member who would be able to legally help a widow in the family. He could marry the widow (a Levirate marriage) so that the line and name of her dead husband would not die out. This also guaranteed an inheritance for her future children (Deut 25). According to Leviticus 25, a kinsman could buy back land that had been sold from the family line. This would preserve both land and family names, both of which had covenant implications in the Law of Moses. The Levirate marriage and the land law provided means by which jeopardized covenant blessings could be regained.

Ruth continued going to the fields of Boaz through the barley harvest and to the end of the wheat harvest around May or June. During this time Naomi, who knew the law, realized that Boaz was their best chance of regaining security, so she made a shocking request of Ruth. Ruth 3:1-5 records that Naomi told her daughter-in-law to go to Boaz in the middle of the night where he would be sleeping at the threshing floor. She was to "uncover his feet and lie down, and he will tell you what to do" (Ruth 3:4).

Naomi asked Ruth to do something that was entirely proper and not inappropriate at all. It was a way for a woman to let a man know that she was available for marriage. It was done privately and in darkness so that if he rejected the proposal no one would ever know or be shamed.

Ruth did as Naomi said and found Boaz sleeping at the end of a heap of grain. She uncovered his feet in a ceremonial act that said, "You can invite me into your life and I will accept."

> At midnight the man was startled and turned over, and behold, a woman lay at his feet! He said, "Who are you?" And she answered, "I am Ruth, your servant. Spread your wings over your servant, for you are a redeemer" (Ruth 3:8-9).

Boaz immediately told her, "Do not fear." But an obstacle existed: there was a kinsman-redeemer who was a closer relative to Naomi. Without touching her, Boaz sent her home the next morning, filling her garment with six measures of barley, or about sixty pounds of grain. By this act, he was telling her, "You will never need to glean again, for I will provide for you."

When Naomi saw the six measures of barley, she knew the night had gone well! Boaz quickly dealt with the closer relative, who declined to purchase Naomi's land and take Ruth as a wife. Ruth and Boaz were married and blessed with a son, thus restoring the property of Naomi and giving both her and Ruth the blessing of continuing the family line.

How can Ruth's story give us strength in the river? Ruth had just lost her father-in-law, her brother-in-law, and her husband, and was left childless, without hope in her economic and social system. She left the only home she had ever known to come to the new and strange town of Bethlehem where she, as a Moabite, would not likely be warmly welcomed. But despite her suffering, Ruth learned to let her godly character shine.

Instead of just trying to get through our trial, we need to stand tall in the river and use it as an opportunity to demonstrate the graciousness that God has demonstrated to us. Even though she lost everything, including her first husband, Ruth maintained several godly qualities.

The Quality of Strength

The first quality of strength Ruth showed was firm resolve and determination. Ruth listened as Naomi said three times in the first chapter, "Go, return to your mother's house... turn back, my daughters... return after your sister-in-law." Ruth 1:14 says that "Orpah kissed her mother-in-law, but Ruth clung to her." Ruth literally wouldn't let Naomi go and refused to be sent away.

Ruth believed so strongly that her place was with Naomi that she demonstrated unwavering resolve and strength of conviction to continue on with Naomi. "And when Naomi saw that she was determined to go with her, she said no more" (Ruth 1:18). Ruth had married into this family and had decided that the best way to survive the dismantling of her entire life was to remain faithful to what was left of her family—Naomi. She knew her mission was to fulfill her duty as a daughter-in-law, though Naomi had freed her from this obligation.

When disaster strikes, one of the greatest temptations is to alter your entire life, schedule, and routine. Many circumstances require change, but the wisdom of Ruth resolves to have strength to continue fulfilling your obligations as much as possible. Ruth was grieving; her world had turned upside down. She was no doubt falling apart emotionally. But if you had asked Ruth what she was feeling or thinking, her answer might have been, "You don't have to fall apart even when you're falling apart." If Ruth would have gone back to her parents it would have meant, "I can no longer go on living my life. I need others to live my life for me." She would have moved back into her old room like a child again.

It's easy to fall for the deception that you can't keep living your life until the crisis has passed or that you have some psychological obligation to stay miserable until answers come. For Ruth no answers were coming that she could see. Even Naomi said so, "But Naomi said, 'Turn back, my daughters; why will you go with me? Have I yet sons in my womb that they may become your husbands?'" (Ruth 1:11). But Ruth was determined to be faithful to Elimelech's family.

If Ruth would have completely fallen apart, it would have been to Naomi's detriment. In the same way, if *you* completely fall apart it will almost always be to someone else's detriment. There is great joy and freedom in keeping your responsibilities to whatever degree you can by the strength God gives. In keeping your responsibilities and having this resolve, you will often find comfort from the Lord in the little things. You may find comfort in the simple act of cooking a meal for your family, cleaning your house, being faithful at work, washing your car, or praying with your children. These tasks take resolve and a dogged determination that if the Lord has given you duties, you need to continue fulfilling them.

Strength is not only something you get, it's also something you demonstrate. For example, Moses summoned Joshua and said to him in front of all Israel, "Be strong" (Deut 3:17). In Ephesians 6:10 we are told, "Finally, be strong in the Lord and in the strength of his might." In almost every single case when someone is told to be strong in Scripture, the definition of strength is "do what you are supposed to do."

The Quality of Dignity

The Hebrew word for dignity means to ornament oneself with honor and quality, or to use a familiar metaphor, to "put your best foot forward." Naomi lost this quality for a time when she played the victim and became decidedly undignified. When Ruth and Naomi arrived in Bethlehem, the women of the town gathered around and were shocked at the sight of Naomi. She had apparently aged considerably more than the ten-plus years she had been gone. Naomi let her grief overwhelm her and, in an understandable moment, let her dignity fall. "She said to them, 'Do not call me Naomi; call me Mara, for the Almighty has dealt very bitterly with me. I went away full, and the LORD has brought me back empty. Why call me Naomi, when the LORD has testified against me and the Almighty has brought calamity upon me?'" (Ruth 1:20-21). "Naomi" means "sweetness," but she instead wanted to be called "Mara," or "bitterness."

    Ruth, on the other hand, maintained her dignity even in her pain. This was not a sense of false pride trying to pretend calamity had not come, but a sense of upholding a dignified calm in the face of hopeless odds. "And Ruth the Moabite said to Naomi, 'Let me go to the field and glean among the ears of grain'" (2:2). This was a humble thing to do.

    According to the Law of God in Leviticus 19:9-10, the poor and the traveler were allowed to follow behind the harvesters and collect what was left behind. Ruth was assertively telling Naomi, "I will glean like the poor and the foreigner." Never once hinting at self-pity or embarrassment of disgrace, Ruth did what she had to do for righteous reasons with dignified humility.

    Later, when Boaz treated her with great kindness, "She fell on her face, bowing to the ground, and said to him, 'Why have I found favor in your eyes, that you should take notice of me, since I am a foreigner?'" (Ruth 2:10). Falling to the ground was not a lack of dignity; it was a display of grace in humbly acknowledging the gift of another. Ruth was neither self-debasing nor self-exalting, but she was adorned with dignity and put her best foot forward.

One of the best speeches you can give yourself in the midst of pain is to remind yourself to be dignified—not a false bravado that pretends pain doesn't exist, but a dignity suitable for one who is a child of the King. Remember, you are one who has been purchased at the cross of Christ, whose destiny is completely secure. Remaining humbly dignified means that no matter how intense your emotions, you won't let unsanctified emotion make decisions for you. When Jesus came to the tomb of His dead friend, Lazarus, "he was deeply moved in spirit and greatly troubled" (John 11:33). But Jesus, knowing the purposes of God the Father, had actually *delayed* coming when He had heard that Lazarus was ill (John 11:6). The emotion He felt knowing of Lazarus's illness and the emotion He knew He *would* feel when Lazarus died did not make His decisions for Him. He knew and trusted the overall plan of God. For you, dignity says that no matter how humble your circumstances, you can be confident of your identity in Christ and God's overall purposes.

The Quality of Wisdom

When Ruth asked Naomi's permission to glean in the fields, she had a plan in mind. "And Ruth the Moabite said to Naomi, 'Let me go to the field and glean among the ears of grain after him in whose sight I shall find favor.' And she said to her, 'Go, my daughter'" (Ruth 2:2). A field could be gleaned two ways; either she could collect in a field that had already been harvested, or she could find a field in the middle of being harvested so that the workers and perhaps the owner would see her. Ruth wisely chose Boaz's field not because she knew who he was, but because the workers were right there in the field. In other words, she made her need known without begging for help. She worked hard, putting herself in a position to form relationships that God might use in her future.

When Ruth met Boaz he was very kind to her. She continued establishing the relationship in humble yet clear terms. "Then she said, 'I have found favor in your eyes, my lord, for you have comforted me and spoken kindly to your servant, though I am not one of your servants'" (2:13).

There is a subtle message here. Ruth had the foresight to express thankfulness in having found favor with Boaz and also hint that she expected his continued favor.

When Ruth had been gleaning in the fields at least a couple of months, Naomi sat down with her and told her to do something radical: get cleaned up and offer herself in marriage to Boaz. "And she replied, 'All that you say I will do.' So she went down to the threshing floor and did just as her mother-in-law had commanded her" (3:5-6). Not only was this an act of submission, but Ruth clearly understood the wisdom in this act. She demonstrated prudence by listening to and following the wise counsel of another.

Our time of testing is an opportunity to act wisely. Ruth is a perfect example of this in the way she accepted Naomi's counsel and, by inference, God's wisdom. We, too, may find the answer to our problem in simply seeking the wisdom of the Lord, not just by praying that God would deliver us from our problem.

The Quality of Kindness

Ruth was known for her kindness—both to Boaz and to the people of Bethlehem (2:11). She had been helping Naomi since the death of her husband. She mourned the death of her spouse by serving and providing for someone else. Ruth was a young woman and her parents were likely still alive. She could have easily been set up with another husband in Moab, but she chose the harder road to purposefully be kind to her mother-in-law. Her actions in the midst of suffering were so extraordinary that everyone was talking about it. Boaz was deeply moved by this genuine example of kindness in Ruth.

Even in Ruth's marriage proposal to Boaz she showed kindness, and Boaz recognized it. "And he said, 'May you be blessed by the LORD, my daughter. You have made this last kindness greater than the first in that you have not gone after young men, whether poor or rich'" (3:10). Boaz called Ruth "my daughter" for a second time as an indication that he knew their age difference and believed that she could have easily caught a young man who could provide for her. Ruth was not only providing for her mother-in-law's daily needs, but she showed kindness in caring for the family line. If Ruth would have married a younger man who was not a kinsman-redeemer, she would have left Naomi destitute, and the family name and land would have been lost!

By asking Boaz to marry her, Ruth ensured that the name of her first husband, Mahlon, would continue, that the land would stay in the family to provide for Naomi, and that Naomi would be restored to her status as family matriarch once again instead of a destitute, old widow. Although Boaz was thrilled that a young woman was wanting to marry him, he immediately recognized that Ruth was serving her dead husband, her mother-in-law, and Boaz, rather than herself first.

But Ruth's abundant kindness didn't stop there. After Boaz and Ruth were married she had a son, Obed. "Then Naomi took the child and laid him on her lap and became his nurse" (4:16). Ruth must have remembered Naomi's bitter words months earlier, "Have I yet sons in my womb?" (1:11). By becoming Obed's nurse, Naomi was formally adopting him not just as her grandson, but as son in the place of her dead sons. Ruth was saying, "You do have a son in your womb! My son can be your son, too!" Ruth even let Naomi help name the child. "And the women of the neighborhood gave him a name, saying, 'A son has been born to Naomi.' They named him Obed" (4:17). As was the custom of the day, the whole town weighed in on what the boy should be named, and he was called "Obed" which meant "worshiper."

Naomi, "sweetness," who wanted to be called Mara, "bitterness," was now called Naomi again by the women of the town… all because of the kindness of Ruth. Despite her life turning upside down with the death of her husband, brother-in-law, and father-in-law, and moving into a foreign country in the middle of her grief while serving her mother-in-law's bitter spirit, Ruth radiated kindness like a spotlight that burst from her soul.

Be like Ruth. Allow the trials and pains of your life to help you become kinder, more selfless, and softer to the needs of others. Perhaps that's the entire point of your trial in the sovereign plan of God!

The Quality of Usefulness

Although it might seem obvious that Ruth was useful, it's worth looking at *how* she was useful so we, too, can learn to be useful for the Lord. Even the field workers recognized this, saying, "She said, 'Please let me glean and gather among the sheaves after the reapers.' So she came, and she has continued from early morning until now, except for a short rest" (2:7). Most likely Ruth showed up at the field at dawn. "So she gleaned in the field until evening. Then she beat out what she had gleaned, and it was about an ephah of barley" (2:17).

After working hard all day, she beat the stalks of barley until she had collected an ephah, which was about thirty pounds. To collect thirty pounds of pure grain (enough for many days of food), she would have had to collect hundreds of pounds of barley stalks. Ruth was doing a man's full day of work! The women of Bethlehem knew she was a hard worker and was useful, as she proved herself to be. They told Naomi, "your daughter-in-law who loves you, who is more to you than seven sons!" (4:15). Seven sons was considered the supreme blessing to a Hebrew family.

It can be tempting in trials to stop being useful, productive, and active. Ruth probably worked harder *during* her time of grief than before it. Being productive and working until exhausted was likely therapeutic and healthy for her. She may have used this time to reflect on her loss or to continue grieving, all while still being useful and productive for Naomi and herself. Oftentimes, grieving people stop taking care of themselves and others, and yet that is the exact opposite of what they should be doing.

The Quality of Fearing God

Now we come to the most important character quality of all: the fear of God. By fearing God you acknowledge that you are a sinner in need of grace and that only through Christ's sacrifice on the cross can your debt of sin be paid. Only then can God's wrath be fully satisfied. Prior to the cross, those who feared God were justified by faith and by the future sacrifice of Christ. Ruth chose to trust that the Messiah would one day fulfill this sacrifice, satisfying the debt of her sin. Her response to her situation demonstrated the fear of God.

When Ruth made her commitment to serve Naomi, it was not just to serve Naomi but to make a profession of full faith and trust in the Lord.

> But Ruth said, "Do not urge me to leave you or to return from following you. For where you go I will go, and where you lodge I will lodge. Your people shall be my people, and your God my God. Where you die I will die, and there will I be buried. May the LORD do so to me and more also if anything but death parts me from you" (Ruth 1:16-17).

Ruth acknowledged the supremacy of God, her worship of God, her submission to God, and her identification with the people of God. The Lord blessed Ruth in at least ten different ways as a reward and sign that He was watching over her:

1. *Ruth "happened" to go to the field of Boaz through God's providential leading.* "So she set out and went and gleaned in the field after the reapers, and she happened to come to the part of the field belonging to Boaz, who was of the clan of Elimelech" (2:3).

2. *God protected and cared for her above and beyond what would be expected of a gleaner.* "Then Boaz said to Ruth, 'Now, listen, my daughter, do not go to glean in another field or leave this one, but keep close to my young women. Let your eyes be on the field that they are reaping, and go after them. Have I not charged the young men not to touch you? And when you are thirsty, go to the vessels and drink what the young men have drawn'" (2:8-9).

3. *Boaz gave her a blessing for her faithfulness to Naomi as proof that she was under the wings of the Lord.* "The LORD repay you for what you have done, and a full reward be given you by the LORD, the God of Israel, under whose wings you have come to take refuge!" (2:12).

4. *Ruth was blessed with a free meal.* "And at mealtime Boaz said to her, 'Come here and eat some bread and dip your morsel in the wine.' So she sat beside the reapers, and he passed to her roasted grain. And she ate until she was satisfied, and she had some left over" (2:14).

5. *The Lord extended extra generosity and favor by Boaz.* "When she rose to glean, Boaz instructed his young men, saying, 'Let her glean even among the sheaves, and do not reproach her. And also pull out some from the bundles for her and leave it for her to glean, and do not rebuke her'" (2:15-16).

6. *Ruth was able to feed Naomi immediately without having to wait for the ripening and processing of the grain.* "And she took it up and went into the city. Her mother-in-law saw what she had gleaned. She also brought out and gave her what food she had left over after being satisfied" (2:18).

7. *Boaz affirmed that her faith was real, since she had shown herself to be a worthy woman of strong of character and a worshipper of the Lord.* "And now, my daughter, do not fear. I will do for you all that you ask, for all my fellow townsmen know that you are a worthy woman" (3:11).

8. *God saved land for Naomi's family line.* "Then Boaz said to the elders and all the people, 'You are witnesses this day that I have bought from the hand of Naomi all that belonged to Elimelech and all that belonged to Chilion and to Mahlon. Also Ruth the Moabite, the widow of Mahlon, I have bought to be my wife, to perpetuate the name of the dead in his inheritance, that the name of the dead may not be cut off from among his brothers and from the gate of his native place. You are witnesses this day'" (4:9-10).

9. *The Lord gave Ruth a husband and provider.* "So Boaz took Ruth, and she became his wife" (4:13a).

10. *The Lord gave Ruth a son.* "And the women of the neighborhood gave him a name, saying, 'A son has been born to Naomi.' They named him Obed. He was the father of Jesse, the father of David" (4:17).

Recognizing these ten blessings God gave to Ruth helps us see the bigger purpose of the Book of Ruth and how God used Ruth's life for an infinitely bigger plan! The book begins in a time of chaos and pain for Israel, "In the days when the judges ruled"(1:1). But the book ends with the hope of David, a future king who would bring order to the chaos. "Obed fathered Jesse, and Jesse fathered David" (4:22).

Every single prayer in the Book of Ruth was answered. God rewarded Ruth's faith and watched out for her in the background as her life fell apart, and He graciously restored and renewed. We must remember that even in pain and suffering the Lord is working behind the scenes on behalf of the one who trusts in Him.

Your faith says, "I will look each day for every little blessing in the middle of this anguish." If you look hard enough, you will see the fingerprints of Almighty God on each day during your time of trial! To those going through rivers of tears, Ruth says, "Let your godly character shine through in strength, dignity, wisdom, kindness, usefulness, and the fear of God."

CHAPTER

7

Paul Says,
"Find God's Power in Your Weakness"

One of the most frequent questions that any Christian faces is, "*How* do I navigate the deep waters of a river of trial, pain, and surprise anguish?" A poor understanding of this issue stems from not being taught adequately on issues such as the sovereignty of God or the effect of the gospel on our present state of mind, and from not *truly* understanding the nature of trusting the Lord.

In fact, being unarmed in the realm of dealing with suffering leads Christians to sin in their attempts to plaster man-made cures or philosophies over their problem. Maybe they believe that God is obligated to do what they want, or they're angry at God, or they're not able to see their trial in the context of a bigger picture. Maybe they're incapable of functioning on a day-to-day basis, grounded in fear, unforgiveness, or some other sinful response, unable to fulfill their responsibilities.

One of the biggest obstacles we face when trials hit us is the emotional backlash that makes us feel like we are drowning in anger, confusion, fear, or a debilitating depression. It is the angst that can feel like someone put a coat of lead on your back, a palpable weight and heaviness of spirit. This can limit your ability to think, focus, or even communicate. Sometimes this is produced by anger that consumes your being, and sometimes it is fear of the unknown and the realization that all you thought was secure is not. On top of all this looms the self-condemnation that, "My faith should be stronger than this!" You're left wondering why you can't control life. No matter the nature of the trial, you are in a place of weakness. What you desperately need is power to stand tall in the river of tears that is all around you.

The Purpose of Salvation

It continues to be popular to seek mystical ways to get power from God. Andrew Wommack wrote an article entitled "Our Authority Releases God's Power" in which he said, "God has already provided His healing power and placed it on the inside of every born-again believer. It is up to us to release it. Understanding and using our authority is the key to seeing miracles happen."[ix] Essentially, this theme has endless variations that all teach the same thing: "Tapping into God's Power," "How to Receive God's Power," "Receiving God's Healing Grace," etc. The problem is that all of these messages operate under the assumption that God's power is something you carry out. It is the idea that you can control your life, do what you want, and not have to care about what God wants.

Receiving God's power to get what you want becomes equated with salvation, and suddenly the purpose of getting saved is to get the healing and the fulfillment that you want. If you believe that this is the purpose of salvation, then you may not have been genuinely saved, because the purpose of salvation is to glorify God by bringing citizens into His kingdom so God can forgive them of their sins before they die. Sadly, billions of dollars have been made writing books and holding conferences on "getting God's power."

On the other hand, the apostle Paul would not have sold many books today. His answer is not exciting and has no apparent instant gratification. He doesn't tell God what he is going to do by supposedly "releasing His power," as if God is an inanimate faucet that you just have to learn to twist the right way. No, Paul's method wouldn't have made it on the conference circuit or on the best-seller list. Notice Paul doesn't say, "Claim God's power! Release God's power! Receive God's power!" or as one author said, "Confidently take hold of God's power with strength!" Instead, Paul says, "Find God's power in your weakness."

Five Legs of the Journey Toward Spiritual Strength

Paul's history with the Corinthian church was filled with both joy and anguish. After leaving his eighteen-month ministry in Ephesus (from the fall of AD 50 to the spring of AD 52), he wrote a letter warning the Corinthians not to associate with immoral people who claimed to be believers. The letter—one we do not have and is not part of Scripture—was apparently misunderstood, but was referred to in 1 Corinthians.

In the spring of AD 56, Paul received a verbal report from Chloe's household, as well as a letter with specific questions from the church. The letter had questions, and the verbal report gave details of various sins that were plaguing the church. So Paul responded right away with another letter, now known as 1 Corinthians. He addressed the hot topics reported by Chloe's household and answered the written questions.

Soon after, in that same spring, Paul visited Corinth. However, the church was unreceptive and he was run out of town. Paul wrote a third letter known as the "sorrowful letter"—another letter that was not part of the inspired Scripture—and delivered it by Titus. He was trying to build bridges and rectify the situation. In the summer of AD 56, Paul left Ephesus and went to Troas to wait for Titus, who would tell him how the letter was received.

Titus caught up to Paul in Macedonia and gave him the good news that the church had softened and received Paul's letter with a positive response! Paul then wrote his fourth letter—2 Corinthians—later that summer or fall of AD 56. In the first seven chapters, Paul described and explained his ministry to clear up any misconceptions and defend against false accusations. Then in chapters 8-9 he addressed the church in his ministry of giving, as he was taking up a collection for poor believers in Jerusalem.

In 2 Corinthians 10, Paul defended and vindicated his credentials as an apostle, which had apparently been questioned by the very people whom he had led to faith in Christ. Paul told them that they had, in essence, forced him to boast, "We will not boast beyond limits, but will boast only with regard to the area of influence God assigned to us, to reach even to you" (2 Cor 10:13).

Paul was saying, "Okay, if you want me to prove my credentials as an apostle, then here's what I'll boast about..." Then he challenged anyone to produce a list of suffering anywhere near what he had gone through: imprisonment, countless beatings, near-death experiences, the requisite thirty-nine lashes five times, beaten with rods three times, stoned and left for dead once, shipwrecked three times, floated adrift on the sea for a night and a day, danger from rivers, robbers, and his own unruly church members, danger in cities and in the wilderness, danger from false brothers, sleepless nights, hunger and thirst, extreme cold and heat, and the daily pressure of responsibility he felt for all the churches.

Then in 2 Corinthians chapter 12 he spoke of visions and revelations from the Lord. He told the story of a man who had a vision of heaven itself (the man was actually Paul, but he told the story as if it were someone else, since he would not blatantly boast that he had seen heaven personally). Because the Lord had entrusted so much to him, Paul let the Corinthian church know about the price he had to pay for this privilege.

The First Leg of the Journey: A Time of Pleading

So to keep me from becoming conceited because of the surpassing greatness of the revelations, a thorn was given me in the flesh, a messenger of Satan to harass me, to keep me from becoming conceited. Three times I pleaded with the Lord about this, that it should leave me (2 Cor 12:7-8).

The revelations Paul received as an apostle were absolutely extraordinary. They were part of God's plan to bring His truth to the newly formed church, but they were *not* the normal experience of a Christian. Paul was a sinner, and the probability of this privilege puffing him up was high. It would have been easy to generate a sense of spiritual superiority or arrogance, so the Lord allowed this "thorn in the flesh."

The word "thorn" has a significant meaning in this context and could be better translated "pointed stake." The word "messenger" literally translates as an "angel" of Satan. Here is the paradox: the stake was the messenger of Satan, but God was the ultimate orchestrator. God's hand never touches that which is evil, but He uses it for His own purposes. This means that God planned some type of terrible suffering to keep Paul effective in his ministry. Paul had been through a lot, but this was near or at the top of his "misery list." The thorn was not a one-time occurrence, but rather was recurring and painful. Paul mentioned that the thorn was sent to "harass" him; this is the same word used of the abuse of Jesus the night He was arrested.

Most likely Paul received this stake in the flesh soon after the Lord gave him the vision of heaven. At the time of this letter, he had been dealing with his stake for the past fourteen years. From the text we learn that the stake had several distinct characteristics. It was given to Paul as a result of the magnificent visions and revelations he had received. It caused him terrible pain either physically or emotionally and happened over and over again. Whatever it was, it was bad enough that Paul begged God for relief. Paul rightly saw it as both a gift from God to keep him humble, as well as an instrument of Satan. We also know it was a permanent condition that would not be taken away, and it caused Paul to feel humbled, weak, and powerless.

So what *was* the stake? There are three major theories. As one writer said, "The proposed identifications [are] legion in number."* It could have been a spiritual or psychological anxiety of some sort, or even anguish over what was happening in the churches. The anxiety might have been a by-product but probably not the thorn itself.

The most popular idea is that it was some kind of physical malady. Paul may have had some type of eye disease, and everything from migraines to fevers to back problems to epilepsy to a speech impediment have been suggested. It is important to remember that it was something that would have been going on for a decade and a half and had to be something that did not interfere with Paul's hard labor or travels. The biggest evidence for this reason is the phrase "in the flesh." However, in the New Testament the word "flesh" could refer to the physical body or just the whole of your personhood.

Another idea is that the stake was some type of opposition to Paul, either in general or a specific person, as a messenger of torment. Every other time Paul used the word "messenger" he referred to angels. In the New Testament, the verb "harass me" was always used in reference to torment coming from a person. Paul prayed that this messenger would "leave him" as a person departing.

Some people think this was an opponent of Paul, a demon-possessed false teacher who tormented Paul's ministry for years. Others believe it referred to a specific false teacher in Corinth—a false apostle who kept tearing down Paul's work. Paul had already rebuked the church in chapter 11 for tolerating false apostles. Another option is that the stake was not limited to just one person but was a tormenting tactic used by multiple people. Paul may have recognized a pattern of torment through an unrelated group of people, all who were aimed at causing pain in Paul's life and efforts for the gospel. However, it was not in the Holy Spirit's plan to reveal what the stake was, so that in this way we can take comfort from Paul's encouragement when we have our own "thorns in the flesh," whatever they might be.

Paul used the Greek word *kurios* to refer to God when he said he pleaded with "the Lord." When Paul used *kurios* he usually referred to God the Father. He most often used the term without the definite article ("the" in English), but when referring to Jesus, he used the article. Thus, these prayers were directed toward Jesus—to the One who had confronted and saved him on the road to Damascus so many years earlier. Paul prayed to Jesus yearning for relief from his stake, unselfishly concerned that it might hamper his effectiveness in ministry. He pleaded with the Lord Jesus three times—most likely three periods of times, not just three prayer times—and was intently focused on appealing for liberation.

Slowly, Paul began to see the spiritual benefit of the stake. At first he begged the Lord to take it away, but later he realized that if God gave it for a reason and it wasn't going away, then maybe it was a good thing. Few people comprehend the immediate spiritual benefit of their affliction. It is rare to find a believer who begins thinking about the spiritual benefits of their trial when the trial strikes. Our default position is, "Lord, take it away!" And yet imagine the Lord's compassion and heartache at seeing the suffering of his precious son Paul. Even though pain is part of the Lord's plan, never think that God is stoic and unmoved at your pain.

The Second Leg of the Journey: The Sufficiency of Grace

"But he said to me, 'My grace is sufficient for you, for my power is made perfect in weakness'" (2 Cor 12:9a). In the Greek wording of this text, Jesus' answer is in a perfect pattern of obvious parallels. The first and last phrases parallel each other while the second and second-to-last parallel each other, but the center is the most important section:

A "Is sufficient"
  B "for you"
    C "my grace"
    C^1 "my power"
  B^1 "in weakness"
A^1 "is perfected"

Jesus wanted Paul to focus on the grace and power of Christ. He reminded Paul that he would be given grace to receive whatever came to him and grace to be content with his situation. In the same way that Paul was saved by grace, he was also lifted up in the midst of suffering by grace. He would never lack what he needed to be more than a conqueror, as Paul himself had written in Romans 8. Grace is not just the unmerited favor of God that saves us, but the force that sustains us throughout our lives. Philippians 2:13 reminds us that "it is God who works in you, both to will and to work for his good pleasure." God's grace doesn't transform the situation, it transforms our *perspective* of the situation.

Grace is sufficient. It's all we need. It's enough. To be "made perfect" is to bring something to an end or goal, to find its consummation. Jesus is saying, "In your life, I am the most powerful when you are the most dependent." Self-sufficient Christians are weak, easily deceived, ineffective in service, easily angered, over-confident, and ruled by their emotions. Insufficient Christians, who know they can do nothing outside the power and strength that Christ gives, are actually strong, because the power of God flows through their utter dependence on Him.

The Third Leg of the Journey: Our External Response

Some of the Corinthians were claiming that Paul was not a qualified apostle, so Paul stopped to refute these public claims by proving his credentials. "You want me to boast? You want me to prove my credentials? Fine then, I'll boast about…" He proceeds, "Therefore I will boast all the more gladly of my weaknesses, so that the power of Christ may rest upon me" (2 Cor 12:9b).

Paul was not saying that "weakness is power," but as an apostle of Christ his weaknesses proved the effective working of the power of Christ in his ministry. That which made Paul seem so weak paradoxically allowed the power of Christ to work through him all the more. Paul was able to boast in his weaknesses rather than pray for their removal. His weaknesses became the vehicle by which God's grace and Christ's power were fully manifested to himself and to others.

Paul boasted, "Praise God for my weakness! I am weak and my total dependence is in Christ, so I can sit back and watch His power fill me and move me and keep me and bless me." Just think, the weaker you are the more you are able to boast in your weakness!

John Piper said it this way, "One key strategy [to magnify the power of Christ in your life] is to identify and exploit your weaknesses." Stop complaining about the stakes in your flesh and start turning them to your advantage by seeing them as conduits of God's strength and sufficient grace. As Piper says, "Don't waste your weaknesses."[xi]

The Fourth Leg of the Journey:
Our Internal Fortitude

"For the sake of Christ, then, I am content with weaknesses, insults, hardships, persecutions, and calamities. For when I am weak, then I am strong" (2 Cor 12:10). Paul was content and delighted in his situation. This was not a delight in pain and suffering, as he still groaned under the load he bore and still longed to get out of the mortal tent of his earthly body as he said in chapter 5, but he knew his sufferings were for the sake of Christ—to be effective in ministry and to become more like Christ.

His weaknesses let him experience Christ's power such that he could even take pleasure in the opportunity. His perspective had been transformed. The stake that was sent by God was the agent of changing him and growing him in trust and faith, thus turning Paul into an even more effective instrument in God's hands.

God gave Paul's pride a complete knockout punch that rendered him helpless and completely dependent, making him very useful to the Lord. Can you imagine a proud, arrogant Paul? How would the churches to which he ministered turn out if that was the example he was setting? Certainly a humiliated and dependent Paul, led forward as God's captive, *accelerated* the progress of the gospel.

To him the stake was now inescapable, and he simply rested on God's grace. This was not going to be a quick-fix miracle. Paul had strong faith in God, and yet His answer was, "No, I will not fix this. I have a different plan that's even better, but I don't have to tell you what it is." The answer to the trial was not deliverance, but grace to bear up under it. What was Paul's definition of strength? "I am *content* with weaknesses." To use our strength in the river metaphor, strength means that the river may hurt but we're fine with it being there. Paul was so content that *he quit praying for his stake to be taken away.*

The Fifth Leg of the Journey:
A Surprising Final Destination

The final leg of the journey to spiritual strength is ironically right where we started. Where is that amazing place of strength you've been seeking and hoping to reach? What is the destination of spiritual serenity, tranquility, and calm? It's right where you started.

Paul began his journey crushed by his stake in the flesh and seemed to be helpless, desperate for relief and answers. But Paul was exactly where God wanted him: in a state of weakness, dependency, and complete reliance on God. "For when I am weak, then I am strong" (2 Cor 12:10b). Paul would be enabled by God to carry out the apostolic calling of service and suffering. When Paul came to the end of his own power and resources, all that was seen was Christ. He realized that if he started his trial at the very end of his own power and resources, then the power of Christ would be visible. Paul was eager to share with the Corinthian church how he learned this great lesson.

About five years after writing 2 Corinthians, Paul wrote to the church in Philippi:

> I have learned in whatever situation I am to be content. I know how to be brought low, and I know how to abound. In any and every circumstance, I have learned the secret of facing plenty and hunger, abundance and need. I can do all things through him who strengthens me (Phil 4:11–13).

Take courage! You, too, can learn to be content; you can be happy with what you have. In our day, perhaps the most widely known champion of finding God's power in weakness is Joni Eareckson Tada. Joni was paralyzed in a diving accident at the age of seventeen, and her decades-long journey as God's ambassador of 2 Corinthians 12:9 has led her to riches of wisdom that we can read about and benefit from.

Joni's impact on the church has been great, and many people should have been moved by the depths of her love and trust in Christ. She has humbly modeled what it really means to trust the Lord no matter what life brings and to be content in any and every situation. Joni Eareckson Tada may very well be the greatest Christian woman author of this era and the greatest writer on the subject of suffering, perhaps in all of Christian history across all generations.

Joni's life embodies the product of living out 2 Corinthians 12:9. Consider her words:[xii]

- "[God] has chosen not to heal me, but to hold me. The more intense the pain, the closer His embrace."

- "Suffering provides the gym equipment on which my faith can be exercised."

- "Heartache forces us to embrace God out of desperate, urgent need. God is never closer than when your heart is aching."

- "Only God is capable of telling us what our rights and needs are. You have to surrender that right to Him."

And lastly Joni said, "Deny your weakness, and you will never realize God's strength in you." Or as Paul would say, "Find God's power in your weakness."

8

David Says,
"Plead With and Praise the Lord"

rayer races to the forefront as a vital part of learning how to deal
with suffering. We have laid a theological foundation that deals
with the character of God, the plan of God, the integrity of God,
and the power of God, but where does prayer fit? Why did this book not
start with prayer?

One, because weak Christians pray weak prayers, and a theological foundation is necessary to strengthen us for prayer. Two, because our default is to pray prayers for rescue before we have understood God's sovereignty, character, and divine right to place us in the river of suffering. And three, immature believers tend to define success as making God do what *we think* He should do instead of aligning ourselves with His will in prayer.

However, we can also go to the opposite extreme of believing that God's sovereignty relegates prayer to secondary importance, or that prayer doesn't really do anything! How do we find a balance? We take the advice of King David who says to us: "Plead with and praise the Lord."

The Context for David's Prayer

When David was just a boy, the prophet Samuel anointed him to be the next king of Israel after Saul. David had slain the Philistine giant, Goliath, and had proven himself a valiant warrior, a loyal follower of Saul, and a man of integrity. He was kingly in every way—a man after God's own heart.

Years passed and King Saul became jealous of David. Saul wanted to kill David and thwart God's plan. David fled to the Philistine city of Gath, and though he was alone his reputation had preceded him. The King of Gath, Achish, received a warning from his advisors, "Is not this David the king of the land? Did they not sing to one another of him in dances, 'Saul has struck down his thousands, and David his ten thousands'?" (1 Sam 21:11). Afraid of what they might do, David acted insane and ran around marking the doors and drooling down his beard. King Achish was confused and irritated by this change in events and told his servants to let David go. What a fall… the glorious hero of Israel was being hunted by King Saul, acting crazy just to survive!

After leaving King Achish, David escaped and hid in a cave near Adullam, a city in the western foothills of Judah. His family joined him there, along with 400 of the dregs of society—men in debt or in some sort of distress. The mighty, rightful king of Israel was stuck living in a cave with hundreds of malcontents following him.

On another occasion, Saul sent 3,000 men to hunt and kill David (1 Sam 24). Saul was camped in the wilderness of Engedi while David and his men hid in a cave nearby. Saul just happened to make this same cave his personal restroom, unaware of David and hundreds of men just inside the inner part of the cave. David's men prompted him to get rid of Saul, so David crept up behind Saul and quietly cut off a piece of his robe. David immediately regretted that he had dared to do even that to the Lord's anointed king, who also happened to be David's father-in-law. In all this David was a monumental example of submission to authority.

> Afterward David also arose and went out of the cave, and
> called after Saul, "My lord the king!" And when Saul looked
> behind him, David bowed with his face to the earth and

paid homage... "Behold, this day your eyes have seen how the LORD gave you today into my hand in the cave. And some told me to kill you, but I spared you. See, my father, see the corner of your robe in my hand. For by the fact that I cut off the corner of your robe and did not kill you, you may know and see that there is no wrong or treason in my hands. I have not sinned against you, though you hunt my life to take it" (1 Sam 24:8-11).

Saul then felt convicted, promised to relent, and went his own way. But two chapters later, Saul was hunting David again with another 3,000 men, this time through the wilderness of Ziph. During one of these times when David was hiding in a cave, running for his life with no place to go, he wrote two prayers—what we now have as Psalm 142 and Psalm 57. Psalm 57 is a prayer in which David balances his cries for help with his devoted, unconditional praise of the Lord. This is a prayer in which he both pleads with God and praises God. David expresses his crisis and his confidence and then comes to a conclusion about his situation.

David's Crisis

David pleads with the Lord in two ways. First, he brings himself to the Lord in Psalm 57:1-3, and second, he brings the Lord to himself in Psalm 57:4.

Be merciful to me, O God, be merciful to me, for in you my soul takes refuge; in the shadow of your wings I will take refuge, till the storms of destruction pass by. I cry out to God Most High, to God who fulfills his purpose for me. He will send from heaven and save me; he will put to shame him who tramples on me. God will send out his steadfast love and his faithfulness! (Ps 57:1-3).

David ascends the steps of heaven, trying to get away from the hopeless situation in which he finds himself. He brings himself to the Lord in the time of trouble in the same way a small child would run to his parents' bedroom during a thunderstorm. His desperation is clear, "Be merciful to me, O God, be merciful to me" (57:1a). Literally, "Show me favor and kindness, have pity on me, be generous, be kind, and show me benevolence!"

David comes to the Lord like a baby chick to a mother hen. He finds himself in a dangerous place—his earthly life is being threatened—so he takes his soul to the Lord, "for in you my soul takes refuge; in the shadow of your wings I will take refuge, till the storms of destruction pass by" (57:1b).

When David writes, "I cry out to God Most High, to God who fulfills his purpose for me" (57:2), there is no symbolic meaning to the phrase "cry out." It means to shout, wail, and moan before the Lord. David shouts aloud to God Most High, for there is no higher authority to whom he can appeal and no safer throne to which he can run. In prayer, he pictures himself under the safe wing of the Lord, warm, protected, and secure.

David both reminds himself and declares to the Lord, "You are God Most High who fulfills Your purposes for me!" In effect, David was saying, "I was just tending a few sheep, minding my own business, and Samuel came to my house and anointed me as the next king of Israel. Don't forget that was *Your* idea, not mine!" In doing this, David was aligning himself with the greatest power in the universe, "You are God Most High, and You are the one working Your purposes in my life."

The tone of the prayer changes, and we see a beautiful picture of a boy going to his father for protection from bullies, seeking the shelter of one stronger than himself for defense. David is safe in the throne room of God, and it's as if he looks around and tells everyone there, "I cry out to God Most High…he will send from heaven and save me; he will put to shame him who tramples on me" (57:2-3). David appeals to God Most High to send out the armies of heaven to help. He pleads with God to show him His strength and to defend His servant.

Seated safely at the Lord's table, David implores God to deploy the panoply of the arsenal of heaven on David's behalf. He has already faced foes in greater numbers and even killed a giant as a boy! But now he is in an impossible situation: a man he has served and loved is pursuing him, the man who is none other than the father of his wife and the father of his best friend, Jonathan. David cannot and will not defend himself, so God is going to have to unravel this knot.

In the midst of crisis, David first brought himself to the Lord. Now he brings the Lord to himself. David gives God a tour of his suffering to show Him his situation. Of course, God is all-knowing and doesn't need to be enlightened, but David is still saying, "Look at what I'm going through here!" He starts out in verse 4, "My soul is in the midst of lions; I lie down amid fiery beasts—the children of man, whose teeth are spears and arrows, whose tongues are sharp swords." "My soul" has a wide range of meaning usually referring to "my life" or "my soul," but literally it is "my neck" or "my throat" and symbolizes where the lifeblood of a person passes. David is saying, "Look what is around my throat, my exposed life and soul—lions, fiery beasts, spears, arrows, and sharp swords!"

Some people feel that the reference in verse 4 to teeth and tongues is speaking of the hurtful words being said to David. It may be true that Saul spoke hurtful words about David, but the 3,000 men pursuing David were not carrying dictionaries—they were carrying weapons. David explains to God that he feels like a helpless man lying down in a cave with his life exposed to lions, fiery beasts, spears, arrows, and swords. David expresses his emotion and his situation to the Lord in clear, vivid terms.

These first four verses teach a clear lesson: when you are up to your neck in the river of suffering, there is a time to make an appointment with the Lord—a time where you need to plead, beg, beseech, implore, ask, and press the Lord. This is a time to *first* bring yourself to the Lord, "Lord, oh how I need to curl up at Your feet and feel the embrace of Your strong arms!" And *second*, it is a time to give the Lord a guided tour of your situation and how you are feeling about it. This is a time to dump every last wish, hope, request, anxiety, and fear into His strong hand. It's a time to cry out to God until you are spent, until you are physically and emotionally drained, and until every last ounce of anguish has been unloaded. This is a time to ask big and believe big—to tell God, "You are God Most High!"

You might need to do this only once, or you might need to do this daily, but do it! Yes, we trust the integrity of God. Yes, we trust the sovereignty of God. Yes, we submit to the will of God. But we never forget that God has invited us to ask, and to ask big. When you have asked, His answer will always be perfect. He might not give you the answer in your lifetime, but "He will send from heaven and save me; he will put to shame him who tramples on me. God will send out his steadfast love and his faithfulness!" (57:3).

David's Confidence

David converses with God like a friend sitting across the table. He has explained his crisis and exposed his human fear, and now he expresses his confidence in God's plan. "They set a net for my steps; my soul was bowed down. They dug a pit in my way, but they have fallen into it themselves" (57:6). David's confidence starts small, but slowly grows. Traps have been laid and a pit has been dug, but ultimately the enemy will fall into it. Having first poured his heart out to God about the difficulties of his suffering, David's confidence in God is returning.

Again he brings himself to the Lord and the Lord to himself. First, he brings himself to the Lord, "I will give thanks to you, O LORD, among the peoples; I will sing praises to you among the nations. For your steadfast love is great to the heavens, your faithfulness to the clouds" (57:9-10). His heart is steadfast—literally "firm" and "stable"—all because of God Most High.

David continues with stronger courage and deeper confidence, "My heart is steadfast, O God, my heart is steadfast! I will sing and make melody! Awake, my glory! Awake, O harp and lyre! I will awake the dawn!" (57:7-8). Here David uses two verbs to communicate his resolve and determination: "I will *sing*! I will *make melody*!" Then he uses two verbs to command himself to do something: "*Awake*, my glory! *Awake*, harp and lyre!" He ends with one more verb of resolve: "I will *awake* the dawn!" as if to say, "I will bring out the sun with my praise!" David is determined to praise the Lord. He reminds us that when life heats up, we must determine to praise God all the more with our whole being.

Back in the cave, David assesses his situation and makes a conscious decision to praise the Lord in the midst of his trial. How can we be ready to praise the Lord in trials? How can we train ourselves to direct our minds to Him as the first thought, first action, and first response to a trial? David is determined to out-praise every trial, primarily through worshipful song. How can you follow David's example? Buy recorded worship music and sing along. Buy a hymnal and sing your way through all the best songs. Take the effort to memorize some choruses and have them ready to sing. If you play an instrument, use it to lift up your heart to the Lord.

Music is a powerful way to praise the Lord. Christian martyr John Huss was executed July 6, 1415. A man named Peter of Mladonovice wrote the details of how John was tied to the stake with ropes and chains. Here is an English translation of what Peter wrote in Latin:

> When the executioners at once lit [the fire], the Master [Huss] immediately began to sing in a loud voice, at first "Christ, Thou Son of the God, have mercy upon us," and secondly, "Christ, Thou Son of the God, have mercy upon me," and in the third place, "Thou who art born of Mary the Virgin." And when he began to sing the third time, the wind blew the flame into his face. And thus praying within himself and moving his lips and the head, he expired in the Lord.[xiii]

In expressing his confidence, David first brings himself to the Lord in praise, then brings the Lord to himself. David lifts his heart to heaven and focuses once again on the earth and his praise of the Lord on the earth. "I will give thanks to you, O LORD, among the peoples; I will sing praises to you among the nations. For your steadfast love is great to the heavens, your faithfulness to the clouds" (Ps 57:9-10).

He is hiding in a cave, running from thousands of men who are looking to kill him. Yet he has an eschatological confidence in end-times. He knows that not only is he going to praise the Lord now, but there will be a day when he will be an evangelist and hymn-singer to the nations. David forecasts a day that he will publically worship the Lord on the earth in the midst of the nations. The next time this is possible will be at the millennial reign of Jesus Christ on the earth.

David understands that ultimate victory is possible because of the character of God. His steadfast love and faithfulness are as high as the clouds of heaven. David began in crisis, pleading to the Lord for help. He continued in confidence, praising the Lord for His promises. And now David comes to a conclusion about how to handle his trial.

David's Conclusion

David understands the difference between what is happening in heaven and what is happening on earth. Although they are radically different now, heaven and earth have an interwoven history and destiny in the plan of God. The glorious end of this relationship climaxes with the sunrise of God's glory over both.

After his crisis and his confidence, David twice prays an eschatological prayer. "Be exalted, O God, above the heavens! Let your glory be over all the earth!" (57:5, 11). In his prayer David foreshadows how the Lord Jesus Himself would teach us how to pray:

Psalm 57:5 "Be exalted, O God, above the heavens."

Matthew 6:9 "Our Father in heaven, hallowed be your name."

Psalm 57:11 "Be exalted, above the heavens! Let your glory be over all the earth!"

Matthew 6:10 "Your kingdom come, your will be done, on earth as it is in heaven."

David's focus has shifted from begging for an immediate solution to looking ahead to the day when the Lord will be exalted over all—the day when there will be no more cares or worry or crying out for help.

Do we plead with the Lord and beg for His help, deliverance, and miraculous intervention, or do we just relax and praise Him, trusting that He will do all things according to His will, looking ahead to ultimate future victory? The short answer is: yes! The long answer is: you can relax in the Lord and praise Him because you have pled your cause, and you *can* plead your cause because you are praising Him and desiring His glory!

As one who has submitted your life to Christ and has asked God to apply the payment for your sin made at the cross, do you realize the incredible position you hold? You can simultaneously have *no* answers and yet have *all* the answers you need! How does David encourage us to have Strength in the River? He implores us to plead with and praise the Lord so that He will be glorified in the heavens and on the earth.

The book of Psalms focuses on eternity. It speaks of the concept of "forever" over 130 times. Here in Psalm 57, David transcends his current circumstances and looks to the day when he will proclaim the gospel and the praises of God to the nations. He is thankful to God and cannot help but praise Him, "You have turned for me my mourning into dancing; you have loosed my sackcloth and clothed me with gladness, that my glory may sing your praise and not be silent. O Lord my God, I will give thanks to you forever!" (Ps 30:11-12).

9

Peter Says,
"Obey the Lord in the Midst of Sorrow"

It was around AD 60, and Nero, the Emperor of Rome, had been in power for seven years. The dark clouds of Rome's first official persecution were beginning to gather over the new church of Jesus Christ, and official hostility toward Christianity was growing as Christians refused to engage in emperor worship.

In the hot July of AD 64, a fire broke out near the Capena Gate and spread quickly across the entire circus, raging completely out of control and destroying nearly half of Rome. The Roman historian Tacitus wrote:

> First, the fire swept violently over the level spaces. Then it climbed the hills—but returned to ravage the lower ground again. It outstripped every counter-measure... Terrified, shrieking women, helpless old and young, people intent on their own safety, people unselfishly supporting invalids or waiting for them, fugitives and lingerers alike—all heightened the confusion.[xiv]

Some citizens tried to help put out the flames, but others reported later that city officials had actually stopped them. People in the mob were seen taking torches and continuing to spread the flames, claiming later that they had acted under orders.

The tyrant Nero heard the news from his palace at Antium and came to Rome just in time to see his own newly-built mansion, the Domus Transitoria, turn into a pile of smoking debris. He at least made a show of concern by organizing firefighters and giving shelter to the homeless, but the fire burned for nine days at the loss of many lives.

The first rumor that spread said that Nero ordered the fire to be started. According to rumor Nero started the conflagration to free up space for his new building plans, and, unfortunately, history shows that he *did* take advantage of the situation to complete building projects. However, to remove the suspicion from himself he accused the Christians in Rome of having set the fire, and the official persecution of the Church began. Soon, it was state policy to suppress Christianity.

Although persecution was supposedly confined to Rome, in reality, attacks on Christians all over the empire went unchecked. The precious believers to whom Paul had written the epistle of Romans were now being arrested. Some were encased in wax and burned alive as human candles to light Nero's gardens, while others were thrown to wild beasts in grim spectacles for great crowds. Many others, including Peter himself, were crucified.

Just a few short years or even months before all this began, Peter wrote to the believers listed in 1 Peter 1:1, "Peter, an apostle of Jesus Christ, to those who are elect exiles of the Dispersion in Pontus, Galatia, Cappadocia, Asia, and Bithynia." These were regions of the Roman Empire that are part of modern-day Turkey. Peter himself was now in Rome, seeing firsthand the growing hostility against Christians that would surely spread throughout the entire empire.

An Encouraging Epistle

Peter wrote to the persecuted believers, but he had a surprising message to share. He didn't tell the suffering and soon-to-be suffering believers to run and hide, protest the government, or pray desperately for deliverance from this suffering. Instead, Peter answered the question, "What do we do while we suffer? How do we handle this?" His answer is unexpected, yet beautiful and simple. His answer is meek and unpretentious, so unlike the Peter of thirty years earlier who tried to cut off the head of the high priest's servant. His answer is so childlike and pure that it defies human logic, yet it makes more sense than anything else ever could.

The question is, "What do we do while we suffer?" The answer, according to Peter, is: be kind to each other. Be honorable to those who hate you. Be good servants to your masters. Wives, submit graciously to your husbands. Husbands, love and be understanding of your wives. Be good churchmen and churchwomen, and be devoted to one another and to the proclamation of the gospel. Or to sum it all up, "As he who called you is holy, you also be holy in all your conduct" (1 Pet 1:15).

More often than not, the suffering Christian (and remember that we all suffer to some degree almost every day) might use suffering as an excuse to not obey the Lord in the way he orders his priorities and treats others. Peter speaks to us about maintaining obedience to the Lord in the midst of sorrow. This is not just a call to responsibility, although that is part of the equation, but it's also a practical way to keep our minds and hearts focused on that which we *can* grasp while in the middle of a river of suffering that we *can't* grasp.

There is a sense of peace and steadfastness that comes with fulfilling responsibilities, tasks that are pleasing to the Lord. In the midst of suffering, Peter offers four concrete responsibilities to be grounded in the Lord. In the classic Shakespearean play *Hamlet*, Hamlet gives his most famous line as he contemplates his own existence: "To be or not to be; that is the question." Well, Peter gives us four things to be. We need to be sanctified, submissive, steadfast, and settled.

Be Sanctified in Conduct

Peter gives four reasons for suffering saints to be sanctified in conduct. First, *for the sake of God's holiness* (1 Pet 1:13-21). "It is written, 'You shall be holy, for I am holy'" (1:16). God is holy, and because you have been purchased by the blood of Christ, God calls you to Christ-like character, even in the middle of a trial. Prepare your minds for action and be sober-minded, setting your hope on the fact that Jesus is coming back and will reveal His full grace at His revelation. Be holy in your response to every trial.

Second, *be sanctified in conduct for the sake of God's Word* (1:22-2:3). It was through the Word of God that you first came to faith in Jesus, "Faith comes from hearing, and hearing through the Word of Christ" (Rom 10:17). For the sake of God's Word through which the message of salvation came, "put away all malice and all deceit and hypocrisy and envy and all slander" (1 Pet 2:1). Instead of sinning, long for the spiritual milk of the Word, which purified your soul to be acceptable to God. Even now the Word sanctifies your soul by helping you grow up into salvation and changes your nature so that you can start acting like a saved person.

Third, *be sanctified in conduct for the sake of God's household* (2:4-8). As a child of God you are part of God's spiritual house. Every house has a foundation, or a cornerstone, and for believers Christ is that cornerstone. All who believe in Him will not be put to shame. But the builders of the house, Israel, rejected their cornerstone, and He became an offense to them. You, however, have believed in Christ and, therefore, have been given the honor and privilege to offer spiritual sacrifices to God through Christ.

Fourth, *be sanctified in conduct for the sake of God's elect* (2:9-12). Remember, you are God's own possession and have been chosen. You have a duty to proclaim the glories of Christ who called you out of darkness. Even while you are suffering, you have been called to preach the gospel. For the sake of those yet to be saved, conduct yourselves honorably among unbelievers. When they speak against you—like in Peter's day when they believed Nero's lies that Christians were the enemy—let them see the righteousness, holiness, humility, and love with which you conduct yourself. Then the gospel will take root in their hearts and they will "glorify God on the day of visitation" (2:12). When Christ returns, those who have formerly persecuted you will now be among you as part of the household of God! Someone once asked C.S Lewis, "Why do the righteous suffer?" His famous answer was, "Why not? They're the only ones who can take it!"

The simple prayer of the suffering saint is, "Lord, help me to be sanctified in my conduct for the sake of Your holiness, Your word, Your household, and Your elect."

Be Submissive in Relationships

Besides being sanctified in conduct, Peter urges us to be submissive in relationships. *We need to be submissive in relationship to government and all ruling authorities* (1 Pet 2:13-16). Peter affirms that human government, even under Nero, is ordained and given by God. We don't need to rescue God from His own sovereignty. Even flawed human governments do some good—they exist to punish the evildoer. The Roman Christians were accused of being rebellious against the government of Rome. Certainly, they would never cross the line of worshipping Emperor Nero, but Peter says to obey his laws and be citizens who take away the false charges of rebellion. Don't use your faith as an excuse to rebel against human institutions. Or, as Peter summed it up in 1 Peter 2:17, "Honor everyone. Love the brotherhood. Fear God. Honor the emperor."

We need to be submissive in relationship to our masters (2:18-20). The Greek word "servants" used here means "house slaves." Peter encourages us to be the model slave whether we have a kind or harsh master because it is a grace to us to endure sorrow while suffering injustice. This begs the question, "In the middle of suffering, the most profound thing I am supposed to do is to be a good employee?" Yes, this obedience to the Lord in submission to your master will bring peace and grace to your life. Peter gives the ultimate example of a submissive man in 1 Peter 2:21-25. Jesus entrusted Himself to His Father in the midst of His suffering by submitting to what the Father had for Him. He didn't return insults or threaten, but He quietly took what was dealt Him and endured it all. He had a greater purpose in mind: to fulfill His mission as our Savior in bearing our sins.

As wives, we need to be submissive in relationship to our husbands. While Rome was heating up and beginning to pressure the church, how were the wives supposed to deal with this impending doom? Peter advised them in 1 Peter 3:1-6 to live godly, submissive lives for their unbelieving husbands and to show the godly qualities of a gentle and quiet spirit. He told them to not be afraid because God is sovereign and would help. And he reminded them to honor Christ by seriously obeying the tasks He asked.

Ladies, when you are suffering for any reason, there is great peace in simply deciding that, "Today, I'm going to be the 1 Peter 3 wife. I'm going to be humble and gentle and serve my husband." This cheerful obedience brings peace and helps you to stop being so focused on yourself and your suffering. But what if your husband is the reason for your suffering? Well, is God sovereign? Yes. Do you love Him? Yes. Then will being a difficult wife make you feel better? No.

As husbands, we need to be submissive to Christ in relationship to our wives (3:7). God calls both husbands and wives to submit to Christ their Lord. Wives subject themselves to their husbands with grace, and husbands devote themselves to understanding and caring tenderly for their wives. Imagine the first century Christian man: "Persecution is coming! I lost my job because I'm a Christian! My children are scared! I need an escape! I need answers!" Peter would have said, "Your wife needs you more than ever during this time of suffering. You need to be there for her."

Married men have faced this conflict for ages. When tragedy strikes they have to both deal with the crisis and deal with the fact that their wives suddenly need ten times the encouragement and love at that same moment. Men, what should we do when we personally are suffering? Show honor to our wives as the weaker vessel. Peter says that she is an heir with you of the "grace of life," speaking of marriage itself, so she should be getting some joy and benefit from your marriage, too. Peter would say, "Stop praying for deliverance from your trial if you don't care about standing alongside your wife. Pray to help your wife through the trial you or both of you are enduring."

As Christians, we can be submissive in relationship to other believers (3:8-12). At the time when you are suffering the most is when you need to be the most gracious toward others. Be unified in mind, sympathetic, tender and loving, and forget the petty squabbles that tempt you to be vengeful and angry. Watch your mouth and keep your tongue from speaking evil of another. Don't hinder God's work in your life by treating those around you badly with the excuse that your situation is the reason. Now is not the time to slack on prayer.

A simple prayer of the suffering saint is, "Lord, help me be submissive in relationship to those in authority, to my employer, to my husband, to my wife, and to all believers around me."

Be Steadfast in Thinking

All suffering happens right between your ears. If you think that what you are going through is hopeless, impossible, and tragic, then thoughts of self pity not based in Scriptural truth and not grounded in the power of God will define your situation. Peter calls us instead to be steadfast.

First, *we should think of opportunities to suffer with purpose.* In 1 Peter 3:13-17 Peter uses various words to describe the need to think. We need to be zealous with purposeful thought about what is good (3:13). We need to be courageous and brave because of our assurance of future blessing (3:14). We need to be prepared to share our faith in the midst of suffering because we know that unbelievers watch us and become curious about this Jesus who changes lives (3:15). We need to be conscientious in our own heart and act in God-honoring ways so as to shame those who think we will fail in sin during a trial (3:16). And we need to be accepting of suffering in God's will because it's okay to suffer for doing what is right (3:17). Peter urges us to think about how to suffer with purpose.

Second, *we should think of the example of suffering with purpose* (3:18-22). Christ suffered to bring the unrighteous to God. Revelation 9 speaks of the bottomless pit where the most vile and heinous of demonic spirits are held until they are temporarily released during the Great Tribulation, a place separate from the Lake of Fire. Undoubtedly, these spirits were thrilled at the death of Christ, perhaps thinking they would be freed soon, but Peter says that Christ proclaimed, to their shock and dismay, that He is alive!

Christ suffered to gain this spiritual victory. He suffered to bring you into the ark of safety in Him, raising you above the fury of the wrath of God. Peter says that baptism, or "immersion," is a picture of dying to sin and resurrecting to life. When we are baptized, we remind ourselves and others that we have chosen to identify with the suffering of Christ, knowing we will also share in His resurrection. We know that every trial has a purpose and a part in the overall scope of God's plan.

Third, *we should be thinking of the benefits of suffering with purpose* (4:1-2). Think about what this suffering is doing for your sanctification: it is accelerating you down the path of ceasing from sin. When you are in a trial your prayers for relief and help and grace focus your mind so acutely on Christ that, at that moment, you are pure, undefiled, and uncontaminated. In your suffering God widens the gap between who you were and who you are in Christ (4:3-6).

In the great hymn "How Firm a Foundation" by John Rippon, there is a famous stanza in which God is portrayed as saying, "When through fiery trials thy pathways shall lie, My grace, all sufficient, shall be thy supply; The flame shall not hurt thee; I only design, thy dross to consume, and thy gold to refine." All that you are suffering is serving to burn away your propensity to sin and to make you more like Christ!

The simple prayer of the suffering saint is, "Lord, help me be steadfast in my thoughts by thinking about suffering with purpose, thinking about my example in Christ of suffering with purpose, and by thinking about the benefits of suffering with purpose."

Be Settled in Church Life

So often we think about faithfulness as churchmen and churchwomen as something we do once we've resolved other issues in our lives. But the faithful church-life of the believer is something we do whether we're flying high above the clouds or battling in the middle of a storm.

It is important to be settled in church life, and the first way to do that is to serve (4:7-11). Peter acknowledges that the end is near, but since it's not here yet, our instructions are to love and forgive each other. We need to be gracious and stop complaining about each other. We need to serve each other. If you are a speaker, then use that gift to encourage. If you are a server, then use that gift by the strength that God gives you. If you are suffering, then serve one another all the more in love and kindness and pour yourself into the life of the church. That's not esoteric, up-in-the-clouds wisdom. It's just plain common sense.

Another way we can be settled in church life is to inspire others (4:12-18). Inspire fellow believers through your gracious response to suffering by rejoicing in trials! Be concerned with sanctification and righteousness in yourself and in the church. Church leaders, husbands, and other leaders need to lead (5:1-4). Peter says, "I'm an elder; I'm witnessing the suffering that is happening and is going to happen, but I'm also a partaker in the glorious future!" While you are suffering, shepherd the flock of God that is among you, and do it with joy. Be an example, and remember, eternity is coming soon!

While the leaders are leading, the sheep need to follow (5:5). If your church elders are suffering, follow! Be humble and acknowledge that God opposes the proud but gives grace to the humble. In everything, be watchful and alert (5:6-10). Watch your *attitude*: be humble now and you will be exalted later. Watch your *anxiety*: cast your cares on Him. Watch your *adversary*: be spiritually strong, be in the word, in prayer, and in fellowship for strength. Watch your *assurance*: the day is coming of restoration, confirmation, solidification, and inauguration, for "to him be the domin ion forever and ever. Amen" (5:11).

The simple prayer of the suffering saint has now become, "Lord, help me in the midst of my time of trial to be settled in my church life, to serve, inspire, lead, follow, and watch." These are the benefits of listening to Peter's admonition to obey the Lord in the midst of sorrow. When you do this, you will gain a purposeful focus, maintain a clear conscience, gain heavenly reward, be surprised by the strength that God can give, and be prevented from being ruled by your emotions.

Peter ends his encouragement by giving one last admonition to stand firm in the midst of suffering. Writing from Rome and wary that his letter might be seized or read by the Roman authorities, Peter sends a greeting from the Roman believers in code, referring to "she who is at Babylon" (5:12-14). Peter's message to the suffering saint can be summed up in the final verse of chapter 4. "Therefore let those who suffer according to God's will entrust their souls to a faithful Creator while doing good" (4:19).

About 250 years after Peter wrote this letter, there were essentially two emperors of Rome: Licinius to the east and Constantine to the west. In AD 313 they signed the treaty of Milan, which decreed that all Roman citizens would finally have religious freedom without interference from the empire. However, Licinius continued persecuting Christians anyway, and in AD 323 the two emperors met in battle. Constantine defeated Licinius. Finally, after twenty-six decades, the persecution of Christians by the Roman government came to an end.

Just two years later, in AD 325 an important church council was held, the Council of Nicea. Here, 318 delegates with their entourages from local churches all over the Roman world came, primarily to answer the heresies of Arius, whose Arian teaching was spreading lies that Jesus was less than God and not one in substance or being with God the Father. Constantine provided lavish and wonderful accommodations for these believers who had been so recently freed of persecution, but the sight of the delegates coming together was almost gruesome. An example is given by the ancient writer, Theodoret:

> Paul, bishop of Neo-Cæsarea, a fortress situated on the banks of the Euphrates, had suffered from the frantic rage of Licinius. He had been deprived of the use of both hands by the application of a red-hot iron, by which the nerves which give motion to the muscles had been contracted and rendered dead. Some had had the right eye dug out, others had lost the right arm. Among these was Paphnutius of Egypt. In short, the Council looked like an assembled army of martyrs.[xv]

Of the 318 delegates attending, only about a dozen had not been maimed for their Christian faith. These wounded men were the ones who denounced the Arian heresy and formally disciplined those who still stubbornly held to it. These were the heirs of Peter's admonitions to the suffering church—and what great men they turned out to be. They understood Peter's admonition to obey the Lord in the midst of sorrow. We, too, can look forward to great peace and benefits as a result.

10

Elijah Says,
"Be Grateful for God's Tender Care"

Is it possible to enjoy life even when sorrow looks on you daily? When your mind feels consumed by the unknown, can the known still bring pleasure? The prophet Elijah answers these questions from the experience of his own personal trial.

When the kingdom of Israel was divided in 931 BC, the once-unified nation split into the southern kingdom of Judah and the northern kingdom of Israel. Since the Davidic kings remained in Judah, Israel appointed other men to be the leaders. In the first fifty-eight years after the kingdom was divided, the northern kingdom of Israel went through eight kings. This next lesson, found in 1 Kings, takes place in about 863 BC and features Elijah, who lived during the reign of wicked King Ahab of Israel.

Ahab had married a Canaanite, Jezebel, daughter of the king of Sidon. Ahab built a temple to the pagan god Baal, assigning hundreds of priests to serve in this temple (1 Kings 16). He did more to provoke God's anger than all the kings who had come before him. Ahab didn't know God and didn't know God's Word, and it was Ahab who fulfilled the curse given by Joshua some 550 years earlier. After destroying Jericho, "Joshua laid an oath on them at that time, saying, 'Cursed before the LORD be the man who rises up and rebuilds this city, Jericho. At the cost of his first-born shall he lay its foundation, and at the cost of his youngest son shall he set up its gates" (Josh 6:26). Ahab ordered the rebuilding of Jericho and subsequently fulfilled that curse. "In [Ahab's] days Hiel of Bethel built Jericho. He laid its foundation at the cost of Abiram his firstborn, and set up its gates at the cost of his youngest son Segub, according to the word of the LORD, which he spoke by Joshua the son of Nun" (1 Kings 16:34).

In the famous conflict between Elijah and King Ahab, Elijah challenged the prophets of Baal. The question was simply, "Whose god will answer?" Ahab, living proof that great evil is not a guarantee of great intelligence, took the challenge. Ahab gathered 450 prophets of Baal and met Elijah on Mt. Carmel as the nation came out to watch the contest. Baal's prophets placed a cut-up bull on an altar, crying out all day for Baal to burn the sacrifice.

Elijah then set up an altar of wood with a bull and ordered that it be drenched in water multiple times. Elijah prayed that the people would once again see and know that the Lord is God. The fire of the Lord came down and consumed the offering, the wood, the water, the stones of the altar, and the dirt around the altar! The faith of God's people was renewed once again, and they fell on their faces proclaiming, "The Lord! He is God! The Lord! He is God!" At Elijah's order, the people captured the 450 prophets of Baal, and Elijah executed them.

Because of Israel's unbelief, God had afflicted the northern kingdom with a long drought that lasted several years. But after God's victory over the prophets of Baal, many people in Israel repented, and God sent rain once again. However, there was at least one person who wasn't happy that her precious prophets of Baal had been slain: Queen Jezebel. Jezebel sent a message to Elijah that she was going to have him killed before the next day was gone.

Instead of a day of triumph, it became a day of terror. Elijah ran for his life! He and his servant fled south from Samaria to Beersheba, running about 100 miles total—almost four marathons in a row! He said a final goodbye to his servant and traveled a day into the wilderness to die. He arrived physically exhausted and spiritually battle-weary.

Elijah believed that despite his best efforts he had failed, and that Baal worship would grow once again in Israel. He believed that there was no one else to represent God and stand for righteousness. His despair was at an all-time high.

> But he himself went a day's journey into the wilderness and came and sat down under a broom tree. And he asked that he might die, saying, "It is enough; now, O LORD, take away my life, for I am no better than my fathers." And he lay down and slept under a broom tree. And behold, an angel touched him and said to him, "Arise and eat." And he looked, and behold, there was at his head a cake baked on hot stones and a jar of water. And he ate and drank and lay down again. And the angel of the LORD came again a second time and touched him and said, "Arise and eat, for the journey is too great for you." And he arose and ate and drank, and went in the strength of that food forty days and forty nights to Horeb, the mount of God (1 Kings 19:4-8).

Just three verses from the end of chapter 18, where Elijah is the strong victorious prophet, victory has turned into defeat and the courageous prophet into a terrified fugitive. Awesome, supernatural things are happening both before and after this passage. First, fire comes from heaven to consume Elijah's sacrifice, God sends rain on the drought-stricken land, and Elijah slays the wicked prophets of Baal. Afterward, Elijah will see a great, strong wind that tears rocks to pieces with an earthquake and supernatural fire. But in between these intense moments of spiritual concentration, we find the unexpected: *a cool drink and a bite to eat.* Food and water—the epitome of simplicity.

God knew precisely what Elijah needed. He knew that Elijah was going through a time of intense, long-range suffering—the kind that demands all of your energy. From Elijah we can learn to be grateful for God's tender care. We don't want to forget to appreciate and enjoy God's daily blessings. Just because you are suffering doesn't mean you have to be miserable.

Enjoy God's Pleasures

Elijah asked God to take his life. This is ironic because the whole reason Elijah ran away from Jezebel in the first place was to *save* his life. He said that he was no better than his fathers. In other words, he felt like he was no more successful than his forefathers in getting rid of Baal worship from Israel. Sure, he had killed 450 false prophets, but the instigator of Baal worship was still on the throne; Ahab and Jezebel were both still in charge.

Elijah lay down under a broom tree and hoped that the Lord would take his life. But in the very place he thought he would die, the Lord allowed him to live. In fact, the Lord gave Elijah two subtle blessings even as Elijah was asking to die. First, God led Elijah to this particular broom tree (or Juniper tree). It was not so much a tree as it was a shrub with a broad canopy. Broom trees can get about twelve feet tall and have very small leaves. From January to April they're covered in thousands of delicate, white blossoms that are fragrant and smell like honey.

Second, instead of dying, the exhausted Elijah fell asleep, slipping into a desperately needed refreshment for his weary body. When a person goes into deep sleep his blood pressure drops, his breathing slows, his muscles relax, and the blood supply to his muscles increases. Tissue is able to grow and repair itself, energy gets replenished, and eventually muscles "turn off," letting the entire body recharge. For the brain, deep sleep is the time when all the information you processed during the day gets organized and filed in the proper spaces. Sleep gives a tune-up to the neurons to get them ready to receive more information after sleep. In other words, sleep resets the body and the mind.

Elijah didn't ask for these blessings, and based on the text we can't tell that he was even particularly thankful for them. But in God's tender care at the lowest point ever in his life, God began by ministering to Elijah with two unrequested blessings.

God's pleasures—the simple, unasked-for blessings that He gives—are evidence of His continued care and concern for us every single day.

For Elijah this wasn't anything earth-shattering. It was just an aromatic, shaded place to lie down and sleep. Imagine if you were in Elijah's shoes and could let yourself just appreciate those little pleasures in life and remember what kind of God you serve. Psalm 16 says of God that, "at Your right hand are pleasures forevermore." Remember, God will never run out of blessings for you.

The best time to look for blessings is when you feel like your life is devoid of them. The enjoyment of God's pleasures is the outworking of a genuine trust in the Lord. This demonstrates authentic contentment. It's the Lord's quiet, comforting way of informing you that He remains right here. He sits with you through the countless silent blessings He gives every single day.

After burying a second son, author Joseph Bayly wrote:

> I was sitting, torn by grief... someone came and sat beside me. He didn't talk. He didn't ask leading questions. He just sat beside me for an hour and more, listened when I said something, answered briefly, prayed simply, and left. I was moved. I was comforted. I hated to see him go.[xvi]

It's good to enjoy a sunset, a walk, a good cup of coffee or tea, or a nap. These are the subtle, unasked-for blessings—God's pleasures. This is the Lord coming to just sit with you.

Enjoy God's Provisions

Elijah may have been finished with himself, but God wasn't done with him. There was still work to be done on Israel's behalf, so Elijah needed strength. Whereas God's pleasures might be defined as the subtle, unseen, and even unnoticed blessings, God's provision consists of the Lord taking care of us in basic ways that at first glance don't seem all that spiritual.

In 1 Kings 19:5 the Lord sent an angel to Elijah. Hebrews 1:14 tells us that angels are ministering spirits sent to serve God's people. Notice the angel's tenderness. He didn't get out his trumpet and blast a wake-up call, he didn't stand ten feet away and yell for Elijah to wake up, but he touched him and brought him gently out of his sleep.

Did the angel say, "You wouldn't be suffering so much if your prayer life was better and if you had decent quiet times in the Word"? Or did he say, "We need to really process your depression, talk about your childhood, and make an appointment with a psychiatrist"? No. He said, "You need to eat."

One of my favorite moments in life is to walk through the door of my home and be greeted with the aroma of something delicious that my wife Sylvia has been preparing. Elijah was hopeless and despairing, but the Lord gave him rest, and hope entered him once again. Right at his head was a freshly baked cake—bread baked outside in the open rather than in an oven—and a jar of water. He didn't even have to move because the bread and water were right by his head; he just ate and drank. Elijah must have needed this tender care. He was so exhausted that he went right back to sleep and slept for a very long time, long enough to be very hungry and thirsty once again.

As Elijah was eating the nourishing bread, this had to have been a gentle reminder to Elijah of the Lord's tender care in the past. In 1 Kings 17, when Elijah had decreed the drought from the Lord to King Ahab, the Lord provided food from the ravens and water by the Brook of Cherith, east of the Jordan River. So Elijah hid at the brook, and ravens brought him food in the morning and evening. But it wasn't long before the brook dried up, and the Lord directed Elijah to Zarephath to be sustained by food and water in another way.

Elijah met a widow there and asked for food and water. She hopelessly told him that she only had a handful of flour and just a little oil, and that this was the last of her food for her and her son. But Elijah told her to fix the bread for the three of them anyway, "For thus says the LORD, the God of Israel, 'The jar of flour shall not be spent, and the jug of oil shall not be empty, until the day that the LORD sends rain upon the earth'" (1 Kings 17:14). At Cherith the Lord refreshed and provided for Elijah; at Zarephath the Lord refreshed and provided for Elijah; and now at Beersheba the Lord was refreshing and providing for Elijah once again.

James 1:17 reminds us that every good and perfect gift comes from above, from the Father of lights, our Creator. This includes the tender, little mercies that sometimes make the difference between a good day and bad day. God gives comfort and help in time of sorrow in multifaceted ways. Don't think that joy in the Lord is limited to a pie-in-the-sky, abstract conceptualization. There is joy in the Lord in His basic provisions! There is joy in the Lord in savoring a steak! There is joy in the Lord in smelling a pine forest!

As an example, one study proved that the scent of pine trees lowers stress hormone levels.[xvii] Another study showed that a natural chemical is released when grass is cut, and that when you smell this, the amygdala and hippocampus parts of the brain (which regulate and slow down the production of corticosteroids) are stimulated, relaxing your stress hormones. Some Australians got smart and actually produced a perfume called "eau de mow" as in "mow the lawn!"

There is joy in the Lord in holding hands with your spouse or your child or parent. One study showed that holding hands decreases anxiety-producing brain activity in the limbic system, the part of the brain associated with emotion.[xviii] Oftentimes those who suffer express that they have either an inability to laugh, since nothing seems humorous, or guilt when they do laugh. This deceives us into thinking that as long as this crisis is occurring, we are obligated to be at the mercy of sorrow and pain.

But who invented laughter? Your Creator did! He made the platypus, an animal with the bill of a duck, the tail of a beaver, and the feet of an otter. On top of that, it's one of only five species of mammals that lay eggs instead of giving birth. And the male platypus has a needle on the back of his feet that will inject venom into its victim… perhaps the platypus has feelings, too!

God created our minds to process information by anticipating what may come next. We finish other people's sentences in our minds because of this anticipation, and when a piece of information surprises us, it causes laughter—the foundation of humor! Someone once asked Albert Einstein to explain the theory of relativity and he said, "When you are courting a nice girl, an hour seems like a second. When you sit on a red-hot cinder, a second seems like an hour. That's relativity." Enjoy a few other things that might make you laugh:

- A successful man is one who makes more money than his wife can spend. A successful woman is one who can find such a man.

- Happiness is having a large, loving, caring, close-knit family in another city.

- Always remember that you are absolutely unique. Just like everyone else.

- We live in a society where pizza gets to your house before the police do.

- Your shinbones are devices that help you find furniture in a dark room.

- The sole purpose of a child's middle name is so that he can tell when he's really in trouble.

- Hospitality is making your guests feel like they're at home, even if you wish they were.

Proverbs 15:13 says that without gladness, your spirit is broken! I have seen on more than one occasion someone in sorrow who is finally able to laugh and laugh and laugh at something silly until the laughter transforms to weeping and into a release of emotion and anguish. So it's okay! Enjoy God's provisions.

Enjoy God's Presence

When the Lord's angel woke Elijah up a second time, he said, "Arise and eat, for the journey is too great for you" (1 Kings 19:7). The Lord still had something for Elijah; his mission wasn't finished yet. "And he arose and ate and drank, and went in the strength of that food forty days and forty nights to Horeb, the mount of God" (19:8). That must have been some high-protein cake! God gave Elijah strength for forty days to go to Mt.

Horeb, also known as Mt. Sinai, even though it was only about a two-week journey on foot.

This contrasted the frantic running that Elijah had finished. It was a slow, take-your-time journey. We can infer from the context that it would have been a time of spiritual refreshment for Elijah, as the next phase of his ministry was about to begin. Supernaturally nourished by the food given by the angel, Elijah enjoyed unhurried time with the Lord.

In the middle of a time of sorrow, our prayer life and our devotional life with the Lord can become hyper-focused on our situation. We've already noted that it is good and needful to cry out to the Lord, to not only praise Him but to plead with Him. But we also need to remember to just enjoy Him. Time with the Lord is safe and secure as you enter the vault of His sheltering presence. This is a time to thank the Lord for His pleasures and His provisions—a time to nestle into His arms and under His wings, to relish the protection of His constant presence.

We love theology because it informs our understanding of the Lord, but theology becomes just an intellectual exercise if it doesn't impact how we worship and how we enjoy the Lord. Do we remember and take to heart that Jesus said, "I will never leave you nor forsake you" (Heb 13:5)? Do we remember that Jesus said, "I am with you always, to the end of the age" (Matt 28:20)? Do we remember that Jesus has given us the Holy Spirit to be our Comforter and Help? Jesus went to great pains to make sure we understand that His presence is guaranteed.

Most of the time my favorite alone-time with the Lord is on Saturday nights as I go to bed. I sense His presence in a unique and marvelous way as I ask Him to do mighty things on the Lord's Day. When you are in sorrow and grief, take time for a brief time-out from begging the Lord for help and think about His goodness, His love, and His might… just enjoy Him!

Enjoy God's Providence

Elijah took his time getting to his next destination. It was a time of reflection and enjoying the Lord. He had come out of his wish to die, but his circumstances hadn't changed. He was still a fugitive hiding from Ahab and Jezebel, and he still felt he was the last prophet left to defend the Lord in Israel. Numerous other times when God wanted Elijah to go somewhere, He gave the command to go to a certain place, but here the angel didn't specify. He only said, "The journey is too great for you."

No one knows where that journey took Elijah, but most likely it was not north where the action was, but rather a southern detour of rest. He may have come to Sinai to somehow connect himself once again with the place where God first gave the Law and where God first covenanted with Israel. When Elijah arrived at Sinai (Horeb), he found a cave and settled there. God said, "What are you doing here, Elijah?" and Elijah replied:

> I have been very jealous for the LORD, the God of hosts. For the people of Israel have forsaken your covenant, thrown down your altars, and killed your prophets with the sword, and I, even I only, am left, and they seek my life, to take it away (1 Kings 19:10).

Yes, the Lord strengthened Elijah, but Elijah still didn't see any hope for Israel. So the Lord gave him a demonstration.

> And he said, "Go out and stand on the mount before the LORD." And behold, the LORD passed by, and a great and strong wind tore the mountains and broke in pieces the rocks before the LORD, but the LORD was not in the wind. And after the wind an earthquake, but the LORD was not in the earthquake. And after the earthquake a fire, but the LORD was not in the fire. And after the fire the sound of a low whisper (1 Kings 19:11-12).

God chose not to manifest Himself in impressive ways, such as the wind, an earthquake, or a fire. Instead, He revealed Himself in "the sound of a low whisper," or as the King James Version says, "the still small voice." Elijah had already seen the obvious manifestations of God's power in the very recent past as the prophets of Baal were obliterated by the Lord on Mt. Carmel.

After the fire, Elijah had apparently retreated back to the cave, because when he heard the sound of the low whisper, he came out of the cave. "And when Elijah heard it, he wrapped his face in his cloak and went out and stood at the entrance of the cave. And behold, there came a voice to him and said, 'What are you doing here, Elijah?'" (1 Kings 19:13). It seems that the Lord chose to make a point to Elijah as he spoke to him in this small, subtle way. God will not always work right in front of you in ways you can see. Elijah didn't have all the information, and he was never given all the information. God basically asked him, "What are you looking for? What are you seeking? What do you really want?"

God gave a marvelous gift. He demonstrated that sometimes He will work in big, dramatic ways, and other times Elijah would need to trust His providential work behind the scenes. Elijah thought he was all alone as a prophet of God and that Baal worship would prevail in Israel, but God had better plans.

> And the LORD said to him, "Go, return on your way to the wilderness of Damascus. And when you arrive, you shall anoint Hazael to be king over Syria. And Jehu the son of Nimshi you shall anoint to be king over Israel, and Elisha the son of Shaphat of Abel-meholah you shall anoint to be prophet in your place. And the one who escapes from the sword of Hazael shall Jehu put to death, and the one who escapes from the sword of Jehu shall Elisha put to death. Yet I will leave seven thousand in Israel, all the knees that have not bowed to Baal, and every mouth that has not kissed him" (1 Kings 19:15-18).

At Mt. Carmel God didn't finish the battle against Baal worship or against the evil kings—he had just begun; reinforcements were coming! We see God's big picture providentially worked out in the lives of many. In the life of Job, we see the happy ending in Job 42. In the life of Joseph, who was sold into slavery, we see the happy ending in Genesis 50. And to inspire those who may *not* see God's happy ending in this life, we have the entire eleventh chapter of Hebrews, filled with godly men and women who saw their happy ending in the life to come.

It is easy to intellectually believe in the sovereign providence of God. We can affirm Romans 8:28 that God works all things together for those who love Him. Intellectually, we can believe that God always gives happy endings to His own children, whether in this life or the life to come. But have you taken a moment to stop and excitedly anticipate the joyous providential work of the Lord? God's providence is amazing!

Enjoy God's Pardon

The ultimate enjoyment we have is the remembrance of the gospel. There is no suffering worse than being excluded from God's family. There is no suffering worse than being an unsaved, unredeemed rebel against a Holy God. We are in the Lord through Christ's atoning sacrifice. Joy in the Lord is a major theme throughout Scripture and is mentioned over ninety times. Psalm 20 says to "shout for joy over your salvation." Why? Because of Colossians 1:13, which says, "He has delivered us from the domain of darkness and transferred us to the kingdom of his beloved Son."

Elijah enjoyed God's pardon of salvation in spectacular ways. When an army of chariots and horses of fire appeared and Elijah went up by a whirlwind into heaven, Elijah experienced God's pardon (2 Kings 2:11). I could imagine that whatever is Hebrew for "This is totally *awesome!*" was dominating his thoughts. When Elijah appeared on the Mount of Transfiguration with Moses and the Son of God in all His glory, I could imagine that whatever is Hebrew for "This is *also* totally awesome!" was dominating his thoughts.

We don't have to feel obligated to live in misery during our trials. We can enjoy life and be grateful for God's tender care. Because of His glory and mercy, we *can* walk victoriously through anything in life.

CHAPTER

11

Job Says,
"God is the Source of Lasting Comfort"

Alex was vital and delightful, full of life and joy in the Lord.[xix] He loved His Savior, Jesus Christ, and was the spiritual and emotional strength of his family. He was passionate about reaching the unsaved with the gospel and generally just passionate about everything he did. He was successful in business, generous in spirit, and a driving force for kingdom work in his local church. He loved physical activity and sports, and used this love to bring the good news of Christ to young people.

And in a matter of minutes Alex went from active and vibrant to taking his last breaths on this earth as an undetected health condition suddenly took his life. His precious family was devastated and, as anyone could understand, almost unable to comprehend the reality of what had just happened. Alex had died about 30 years sooner than anyone expected.

When suffering comes particularly in this sudden unexpected fashion, it can become difficult to comprehend even basic information. Your senses get overloaded with emotion and even confusion. Just making basic decisions about daily functioning can seem overwhelming and engulfing.

And during this time you have a most desperate need for comfort and relief. The feeling that you can't escape your own heaviness of heart can overcome you. I know this feeling well and have experienced it more than once in my own life. The color drains out of life and despair invades your heart like a wicked thief that you can't stop.

If you are so blessed to have a loving family and church family supporting you, this can make all the difference. The comfort given as God's gift from those around us is an indispensable part of walking through suffering (2 Cor 1:3-4). But often, human comfort can be tainted with confusion. The off-handed insensitive comment by one or the quick-fix theological clichés of another can be laced with truth and yet sting and ultimately just further your emotional and spiritual confusion. Or perhaps as so often happens after a funeral, the flood of comfort that came your way for a short time suddenly evaporates as others must move on with their lives.

The gift of human comfort is a vital part of God's gracious help in the midst of your suffering. We must never overlook or undervalue the role we play in comforting one another in times of suffering and need. And we must also remember that when comfort comes, or when it *fails* to come, ultimately *God is the infinite and eternal source of comfort*. This is the lesson that the familiar Old Testament figure, Job, gives to us in the middle of our trial.

Job's Trials

Job lived at about the time of Abraham. He feared God and turned away from evil. The Lord blessed him with immense wealth, seven sons, and three daughters. Each son possessed great wealth. Each had a house of his own big enough and with enough servants that the sons and daughters would feast each day at a different son's home.

God chose Job as an instrument to glorify Himself, and it all started with Satan's accusation against God. Satan reasoned that men like Job only worshiped God because He blessed them, and that if God took away everything, Job would curse God and turn away. Satan was questioning the permanence of salvation and arguing that there was really no such thing as a steadfast, enduring worshiper of God.

God said to Satan, "Have you considered my servant Job?" (Job 1:8). At that moment, Job didn't know it, but life was about to change. God chose to use Job as an object lesson that true worshipers will always be true worshipers, no matter what affliction may come upon them. So God gave Satan permission to afflict Job.

Job's children died, his servants and the servants of his sons died, and his animals were either carried off or killed. In shocked grief, Job responded simply, "'Naked I came from my mother's womb, and naked shall I return. The LORD gave, and the LORD has taken away; blessed be the name of the LORD.' In all this Job did not sin or charge God with wrong" (Job 1:21-22).

Satan was still determined to prove God wrong. "Take away his health and Job will curse You to Your face," he argued (2:5). So God allowed Satan to afflict Job with what was probably the most dreaded disease of the ancient world: an extreme form of leprosy. Job used a piece of broken pottery to scrape his diseased skin as he sat on an ash heap in complete agony and despair. He had lost everything and was now a social outcast. His wife was no help but instead advised him to curse God. "But he said to her, 'You speak as one of the foolish women would speak. Shall we receive good from God, and shall we not receive evil?' In all this Job did not sin with his lips" (2:10). Satan had failed yet again.

Although Job is the main concern in the book, the heart of this Old Testament poetic true-story account focuses on the dialogue which unfolds between Job and four of his friends, Eliphaz, Bildad, Zophar, and Elihu. One might think that these four friends and the significant space devoted to their speeches could clarify the situation and give comfort to Job. Ultimately, however, regardless of how well-intentioned they were, these friends served just to add confusion and bewilderment to the situation. Though all of them spoke some things which were true, they also operated under faulty assumptions which just muddied the spiritual waters and did nothing to give Job the comfort he desperately needed.

The Confusing Comfort of Job's Friends

If you are at all familiar with the book of Job, you know that a large portion is devoted to the speeches of Job's friends. In a moment, we're going to examine how confusing and finally unhelpful these friends were overall. But at the outset, it's important to say what the lesson of Job's friends is *not*. The impractical involvement of Job's friends does *not* teach us that human comfort and the support of the loving body of Christ possesses no value. To the contrary, the bolstering practical influence of brothers and sisters in the Lord can help us make it through the darkest weeks and months of our lives. Our Christian family can make so much practical difference through down-to-earth help and care. God has called us to mutual comfort and concern, and He empowers such needed help. But the deep consolation, the peace that surpasses all understanding, the sense that God is so completely in control that fear and doubt begin to ease into the rearview mirror—this comfort is mediated by God Himself.

In Job chapter 4, Eliphaz gives his speech to Job. He makes some sound theological statements that are generally speaking true. He makes a correct assessment of God's holy indignation against sin. He says that the wicked perish by the breath of God and the blast of his anger (Job 4:9 – 10). He correctly assumes that in his own power a mere man cannot be pure and righteous before God (4:17). He says that the answer to the dilemma of trouble is to seek God and commit one's ways to Him. He rightly says that God "does great things... marvelous things without number" (5:9).

But Eliphaz mixes sound theology with some faulty assumptions which are no help to Job. He gives evidence from his own observations of life that suffering must always be the result of sin. He tells Job that "those who plow iniquity and sow trouble reap the same" (4:8). Eliphaz, seemingly insensitive to Job's recent losses, even says tactlessly "I have seen the fool taking root, but suddenly I cursed his dwelling. His children are far from safety; they are crushed in the gate, and there is no one to deliver them" (5:3 – 4). Job, having just lost his children, must listen to Eliphaz say that Job must be *a fool*, one who has somehow rebelled against God. And when Job protests that he is a fragile man and cannot stand up under whatever it is that God is doing, Eliphaz scathingly accuses Job of rejecting God and sinning with his mouth (15:1 – 6).

And Job, uncomforted, expresses his heaviness of heart and rebuts that he has "not denied the words of the Holy One" even though "the terrors of God are arrayed against me" (6:10, 4). Job believes this suffering is the work of God and yet has not denied God or rebelled against Him. Eliphaz gave Job no hope, no solace. Instead, he just gave condemnation.

Maybe Bildad would have something more useful to say to give Job comfort? Like Eliphaz, he makes true theological observations. He discerns rightly that God is perfectly just in all matters (8:3). Concerning the unbeliever, he correctly states that ultimately the one who does not trust in the Lord has no hope and will perish (8:13). But also like Eliphaz, Bildad jumps to faulty conclusions. In chapter 7, Job expresses feeling as though God has targeted him for no reason (7:20). Though Job is certainly not sinless, he has a point. Job feels as though he is being treated as a wicked unbeliever but cannot see behind the scenes of heaven that God has in fact *boasted* of Job to Satan as being upright and faithful. And how does Bildad respond to Job's legitimate questions? He calls Job's words "a great wind" (8:2) and proceeds to tell Job that God is punishing him for some sin and Job should repent forthwith. In fact, in his second speech, Bildad gives a lengthy review of how God punishes the wicked and places Job in this category. Bildad gives no hope, just guilt and blame.

Surely, as they say, three is a charm and Zophar will offer genuine hope for Job. He makes some astute observations about God, such as the limitlessness of God's understanding and wisdom (11:7 – 9). He also notes God's all-knowing nature in that the sins of men cannot be hidden from God (11:11). But following the lead of Eliphaz and Bildad, Zophar lays the blame for suffering right at Job's feet. Zophar counsels Job to prepare for great confession of sin (11:13) and to get rid of the injustice that certainly must be in Job's household (11:14). In his second speech, Zophar even complains that Job has offended *him* (20:3) and claims for himself great wisdom and spiritual authority to explain Job's situation. Zophar's explanation? The truly wicked people of earth enjoy momentary happiness, but they quickly fall because of their sin. Graphically, Zophar says "though his height mount up to the heavens, and his head reach to the clouds, he will perish forever like his own dung" (20:6 – 7). And the implication he makes, of course, is that Job's true character has been revealed by God's punishment of his sin. Assuming Job to be the cause of his suffering, Zophar counsels Job that if only he will repent, all of Job's misery will be forgotten and even the memory of the trial will evaporate (11:15). For yet a third time, Job is left comfortless.

After Job's three friends have finished their unhelpful advice, a fourth younger man, Elihu, then weighs in on the situation. Interestingly, he discounted what the first three said, even expressing his disappointment that those older than him had so little insight (32:9). Like the other three, Elihu offered theological truths. He attributes all life and ability to God alone (33:4) and observes that mankind needs a mediator between him and God to deal with man's sin (33:23). He voices his belief in the complete perfect holiness of God (34:10). He extols the greatness of God's unfathomable power and majesty (37:1 – 4), He even speaks of the redemption of sin God offers men by means of a ransom (33:28, 24). To our New Testament ears, Elihu makes a lot of sense. A case could be made that Elihu had more to offer than the other three friends, but neither did Elihu succeed in bringing comfort. He accuses Job of spiritual ignorance when he says that "Job opens his mouth in empty talk; he multiplies words without knowledge" (35:16). And though Elihu made some true theological statements, he would not have won any prizes for compassion or pastoral care. Like the three older men before him, Elihu leaves Job only with denunciation and without authentic consolation.

Ultimately, Job rightly assesses the inadequate help given by his friends when he says, "I have heard many such things; miserable comforters are you all" (16:1). At the end of all the multiple speeches of four friends, both Job and the reader are left with utter confusion: right theological statements mixed with condescending blame which add up to no solace whatsoever. Job *never* receives the comfort he needed so greatly. Instead, confusion and spiritual murkiness seems to win the day.

What We Learn From Job's Friends

Interestingly, probably the best thing that Job's friends did came right at the beginning of Job's trial. Job 2:11 – 13 records that Eliphaz, Bildad, and Zophar decided to "come to show him sympathy and comfort him" (v.11). When they saw Job from a distance, his appearance must have been shocking to them because they didn't recognize him. Sharing in his pain and agony, they wept loudly, even tearing their own clothing in grief and pouring dust on themselves as a sign of great empathetic mourning. Then amazingly, they sat with Job for a *full week*, day and night, not speaking a word to him. They saw how greatly Job suffered so they kindly and respectfully just sat with him. Had we no knowledge of the unhelpful speeches that were coming, we would think Job's friends to be a shining example of Romans 12:15 which commands us to "weep with those who weep."

And yet their intention to "show him sympathy and comfort him" (v.11) crashed. Whether they intended to be hurtful and accusatory or whether their good purposes became marred by their own biased sinfulness, we don't know. What we do know is that after all their talk, Job possessed no relief and was arguably *more* depressed. Yet the unhelpful speeches of Job's friends are inspired by the Holy Spirit in the inerrant text of Scripture. These friends are there for a reason: they leave Job and the reader completely dumbfounded as to how to find comfort and solace in the worst trials humans can face. We're left at the end of chapter 37 with a sense of dissatisfaction and hopelessness. If the very best of friends fail to offer true lasting living hope, then what prospect does the suffering saint have of finding the longed-for emotional and spiritual relief in the midst of an unsolvable anguish?

Enter True and Living Hope

Something better had to happen for Job to receive authentic comfort. Something that transcends human opinion concerning suffering. Something certain, true, reliable and powerful. And this something is what the entire book of Job builds up to: *God speaks.*

And it is *only* when God speaks that Job receives genuine comfort. To be certain, Job has had some issues in his response to his tremendous trial, responding at times with frustration or despair. And thus, when God finally speaks beginning in Job 37, there is definitely an element of correction with Job. But it is the correction of a loving Father whose ultimate aim is to demonstrate that *He* is Job's answer. He remains the only hope for Job's consolation.

The correction that God would give Job might seem almost like kicking a man when he is down. But God is cleansing and pointedly working to bring Job to the place that none of his human friends could bring him: *authentic and lasting comfort.*

God's Fatherly Speech to Job

"Then the LORD answered Job out of the whirlwind and said: 'Who is this that darkens counsel by words without knowledge? Dress for action like a man; I will question you, and you make it known to me'" (38:1-3). Because Job was thoroughly convinced, and rightly so, that God was not arbitrarily punishing him for sin he knew nothing about, Job implied in chapters 10 and 31 that perhaps he has the *right* to press his case with the Lord.

So God asks Job if he is qualified and capable of taking the Almighty to court: He asks pointed questions: Were you there when I made the earth? How did I do it? Did you see how I made the oceans? How does light work? What is under the earth? What is at the bottom of the ocean? If you *do* know how light works, how do you turn it on and off? Can you make snow and hail and wind and rain? What do you do with it when it's not coming down? Do you make sure the stars stay on their courses? Can you control the weather? Can you communicate to animals that rain is coming? When there is a drought, can you bring rain? Do you feed all the lions and the baby birds? Are you the one making sure that animals give birth at the right time and in the right place? Can you make a wild ox suddenly docile and willing to serve? Do you understand the strange ways of an ostrich, on the one hand so dumb that she steps on her own eggs, and on the other hand so elegantly speedy that she laughs at the horse and his rider? Did you make the horse strong and mighty? Did you make the hawk and the eagle to fly?

God made his point. He is sovereign and Job is not. At this juncture Job decides it would be better to stop talking, so he says, "Behold, I am of small account; what shall I answer you? I lay my hand on my mouth. I have spoken once, and I will not answer; twice, but I will proceed no further" (40:4 – 5). But Job simply being quiet was not what the Lord sought to give Job. God desired to issue Job utter satisfaction, contentment and ease with whatever He brought to him. God didn't want Job silent or neutral; God wanted Job comforted and trusting unreservedly in the good sovereign wisdom of his God.

So God continued. He asks Job if he has what it takes to take God to court. "Then the LORD answered Job out of the whirlwind and said: 'Dress for action like a man; I will question you, and you make it known to me'" (40:6-7). God asks Job how mighty and glorious he is, "Adorn yourself with majesty and dignity; clothe yourself with glory and splendor. Pour out the overflowings of your anger, and look on everyone who is proud and abase him" (40:10-11). He asks if Job can create a behemoth, a beast of beasts. The best description of this animal is as a type of dinosaur, one of the first of the works of God... the greatest, mightiest animal... a grass eater with a tail like a cedar tree and limbs of iron... who can stand in a raging river and not even notice (40:15-24). God asks Job in hyperbole something to the effect of, "Why don't you capture a behemoth to show me how mighty you are? Or would you prefer the Leviathan?" The Leviathan had skin like layers of armor that couldn't be penetrated with sword or arrow. "Out of his mouth go flaming torches; sparks of fire leap forth... flame comes forth from his mouth" (41:19, 21). This beast crushed iron like straw and pulverized stones like dust. He swam in the sea and left boiling, white wakes in his path. God uses exaggeration to make His point to suggest that if Job is mighty enough to bring God to court, perhaps he might *capture a dragon first.*

Job sat in a hopeless situation, having lost all in this life that meant anything to him. He had gotten no relief from the counsel of His friends, and now God seemed to be *really* coming down hard on him! But God intended Job's good and well-being. Whatever was left of any pride Job may have battled with was gone—utterly crushed, reminding Job that he had no lasting resources or comfort outside of God Himself.

God Brings Authentic Comfort

Humbled, Job acknowledges God's sovereign power and right to do as He pleases. "Then Job answered the LORD and said: 'I know that you can do all things, and that no purpose of yours can be thwarted'" (42:1-2). Job repeats God's first question and confesses that he has spoken out of turn, "'Who is this that hides counsel without knowledge?' Therefore I have uttered what I did not understand, things too wonderful for me, which I did not know" (42:3).

Job repeats God's second question, "Hear, and I will speak; I will question you, and you make it known to me" (42:4). Job acknowledges that through his trial and through what God taught him in the midst of the trial, his knowledge of God leapt forward. "I had heard of you by the hearing of the ear, but now my eye sees you" (42:5). God has orchestrated all the events in Job's life, all the suffering, all the confusing unhelpful comfort of friends, and finally this last overwhelming speech to whittle down Job's list of resources to precisely *one*: God alone. And God's purpose for Job was accomplished. God created a *satisfied, content* man who now had broken through to receive full and complete authentic comfort from God. How do we know this?

In 42:6, the climactic moment of the book, Job said, "Therefore I despise myself, and repent in dust and ashes" (42:6). The word "repent" can mean "to be sorry," and there is an element of that in this case, but this particular Hebrew form of the word means "to be comforted, consoled, and soothed." This is conceivably the key to the whole book of Job. The point of the book is that *wisdom and comfort are found in knowing and trusting God as He has revealed Himself—even when you can't understand the reason for your suffering.*

Job could now sincerely say, "I am consoled and content while I sit in the dust and ashes of my grief and sorrow. I'm now satisfied with whatever the Lord, who alone is sovereign, chooses to do." Throughout the entire book, Job was distressed with internal anguish, but he finally comes to a divinely profound refreshing rest!

Coming to Peace in the Ash Heap

If you have experienced or are experiencing an ash heap situation in your life, it can be tempting to try to find comfort anywhere possible. For some it may be resorting to sinful indulgences to try to drown out pain. For others, it may be desperately seeking reasons that only God knows. For still others, human comfort might seem to be the highest resource possible. Job is a monument to us and an example of a tremendous powerful ability that only God has: *to make the ash heap acceptable.* To bring peace, consolation and comfort when no solution seems to be on the horizon.

God knows how badly you are hurting. He knows the tears, the crying, the screaming out in your heart against a pain you so badly want to escape. What he wants *us* to know is what the Apostle Paul calls the peace "which surpasses all understanding, which will guard your hearts and your minds in Christ Jesus" (Phil 4:7). God wants you to surrender—to acknowledge and lean on the fact that only *He* can offer authentic comfort. Might I suggest the following to help you receive that comfort in your most desperate time of need?

- *Use the book of Job as comfort.* Job was not given just to make lofty theological observations about suffering and the sovereignty of God. Job is given to mirror your experience and to follow the same path that your life has taken: Calamity, confusion, and comfort. Read the whole book in one sitting. Then do it again the next day. The Lord gave you this book as an empathizing friend that tells you that God gets your pain.

- *Use the speeches of God to Job.* Certainly there is a corrective flavor to God's speeches to Job, but remember that God was moving Job toward a specific point: the point of utter trust and relief. God's speeches to Job reminded Job that his heavenly Father is infinitely big, wise and capable. As God gets bigger and bigger in your mind and heart, your trial will get smaller and smaller.

- *Surround yourself with believers who will* not *be like Job's friends.* God also gives comfort through the local church and through believing friends. Don't be afraid to ask someone or even a group to come alongside you in practical ways. In a recent time of pain in our own family, we simply chose a group of people that we asked to be our support system through our own river of suffering. They have been an indispensable part of God's authentic comfort and have demonstrated the love of God to us tangibly.

- *Remember Christ.* When the Apostle Paul was giving comfort to a young pastor Timothy, he exhorted Timothy in 2 Timothy 2:8 simply to "remember Jesus Christ." Follow Jesus once again on the blood-dripping path to the cross. Listen to His agony as the nails are cruelly forced into his body. Watch the sickening thud as the cross is dropped suddenly into a hole in the ground. Feel the hopelessness of our dear Savior as He cries out, "My God, My God, why have you forsaken me?" (Mark 15:34). Christ endured for your salvation more suffering than you ever will. And because of this you have confidence that God in Christ has perfect understanding of your pain and is fully able to sympathize with your weakness (Heb 4:15).

God graciously restored the fortunes of Job, giving him twice as much as he had before, blessing his latter days more than his former days. But the major lesson of Job is not to simply look ahead to God's eventual restoration in this life or the life to come, although that is important. The lesson of Job is that when God reduces you down to looking to Him and Him alone for true relief, you can have complete peace for as long as is necessary. For Job, the trial and the subsequent wrestling with his situation systematically narrowed the focus of Job's life until, seated on the ash heap of his suffering, *all he had left was God*—and he discovered that God was the only authentic source of comfort, God who had never once left him alone but was lovingly seated right by him the whole time.

CHAPTER

12

David Says, "Use Your Suffering for Self-Examination"

For us as regenerate believers in Jesus Christ, we don't have signs or indicators that explain why a certain trial has come upon us. For example, if you break your leg, miraculous writing doesn't appear on the cast saying, "You've been too busy; it's time to slow you down." If your child is rejecting your attempts to steer him toward the gospel, God doesn't FedEx you a T-shirt to wear that says, "Remember when you set fire to your mother's kitchen when you were eight years old?" If you lose your job, your company doesn't send you a letter saying that God told them to let you go so that you could learn to trust the Lord more.

On the other hand, we tend to reject the notion that our suffering is related to something the Lord wants to do in our lives, or that it may be related to an area of stubbornness or rebellion that we are avoiding. The author of Hebrews sets the standard, "In your struggle against sin you have not yet resisted to the point of shedding your blood" (Heb 12:4).

The Lord helps you in progressive sanctification and in your process of becoming more like Christ. The author goes on to encourage us that the Lord disciplines every child He loves—that's all of us—so that "we may share his holiness. For the moment all discipline seems painful rather than pleasant, but later it yields the peaceful fruit of righteousness to those who have been trained by it" (12:10-11).

James 5 speaks of a sick person asking the elders of the church to pray with him to be healed. It's not that the elders have magical healing powers, but rather this person has been in some sort of rebellion, was sick as a result, has now owned up to it, and is making things right with the leadership of the church. There are many wonderful by-products from suffering that we have already learned. Suffering:

- *Draws us to the Word of God:* "It is good for me that I was afflicted, that I might learn your statutes" (Ps 119:71).

- *Draws us to prayer:* "O LORD, all my longing is before you; my sighing is not hidden from you" (Ps 38:9).

- *Produces a greater need for fellowship and mutual care among believers:* "Encourage the fainthearted, help the weak" (1 Thess 5:14).

- *Produces spiritual strength and faith:* "Count it all joy, my brothers, when you meet trials of various kinds, for you know that the testing of your faith produces steadfastness" (Jas 1:2-3).

- *Produces greater assurance of salvation:* "In this you rejoice, though now for a little while, if necessary, you have been grieved by various trials, so that the tested genuineness of your faith—more precious than gold that perishes though it is tested by fire—may be found to result in praise and glory and honor at the revelation of Jesus Christ" (1 Pet 1:6-7).

For your specific situation, this is an opportunity for deeper reflection and self-examination. You probably won't figure out the exact "why" of your suffering, but you *will* do some spiritual cleaning in the meantime.

Our next lesson comes from David, author of many inspiring, encouraging, and comforting psalms. Psalm 38 is a penitential psalm, covering the concept of confession of sin. It is a prayer of self-examination and reflection. At some point in David's history, he suffered from a crippling disease that led him to the point of despair. He was overwhelmed by guilt and a sense of abandonment, but he expressed his desire for renewed fellowship with the Lord. David operated under the assumption that his illness was the discipline of the Lord. Because the text was inspired by the Holy Spirit, we know that David was right in his conjecture. His illness was severe enough to cause David to intently examine not only his situation, but his own heart as well.

Psalm 38 can be broken into a dramatic series of prayers with a personal reflection in between each prayer. Picture a man kneeling before the Lord in prayer, then getting up, talking to himself, reflecting on his situation, then going back to kneel in prayer, then getting up, and so on. This is the picture Psalm 38 gives us. David is trying to answer one basic question: Can those who place their faith in the Lord pray with confidence to be delivered from severe discipline when they repent of sin?

First Prayer: A Request for Reconciliation

O LORD, rebuke me not in your anger, nor discipline me in your wrath! For your arrows have sunk into me, and your hand has come down on me. There is no soundness in my flesh because of your indignation; there is no health in my bones because of my sin. For my iniquities have gone over my head; like a heavy burden, they are too heavy for me (Ps 38:1-4).

David is fully aware of God's sovereign work in his life. Not all disease is associated with individual sin, but David is clear that in this case, there is a definite cause and effect. He speaks of "Your anger... [and] your wrath" with the sense of indignation against disobedience (38:1). He feels weighed down by his own guilt. "Your indignation... my sin... my iniquities... [are] a heavy burden" (38:3-4). David emphasizes with word pictures of piercing arrows and smashing fists how deeply God had wounded him (38:2).

In verse 3, David describes his state of complete incapacitation as "no soundness in my flesh [and] no health in my bones." This is not just a headache or sore throat, but David speaks of his whole person, weakened to the point of uselessness. There is a sense of being overwhelmed by the seriousness of his sin as if he knows, or at least suspects, the reason for discipline. In any case, his guilt is heavy, and he begins to list specific reasons of why God might be intervening (38:4).

It is important to note that in David's opening prayer, he never questions the justice of God but instead recognizes that if God is disciplining him, the reason must be "because of my sin" (38:3).

First Reflection: David's Physical Situation

My wounds stink and fester because of my foolishness, I am utterly bowed down and prostrate; all the day I go about mourning. For my sides are filled with burning, and there is no soundness in my flesh. I am feeble and crushed; I groan because of the tumult of my heart (Ps 38:5-8).

Similar to Job's disease, David has some type of wounds or sores and some kind of infectious discharge, but his disease is never officially diagnosed (38:5). David takes responsibility for his situation and knows that this is happening to him "because of my foolishness" (38:5). He is "utterly bowed down and prostrate," perhaps writhing, convulsing, or having seizures, in addition to being humiliated through his sickness as he responds to great pain (38:6).

When David says that his "sides are filled with burning," he is most likely referring to his muscles and kidney area, so it could have been some kind of backache or an inflammation causing pain in his abdomen (38:7). Either way, he feels "feeble" or "weak and cold," and groans, literally "roars," from internal pain and grief that translated into an incoherent cry (38:8). Skipping ahead to verse 10, David experiences a rapid pulse, at times mixed with weakness and blurred vision.

Piecing this puzzle together, we understand that David is convulsing with inflamed, oozing sores, having trouble with his eyesight, and suffering from weakness and cold, his pulse racing at times. This is clearly a serious physical condition that is affecting every function of his body. David's first reflection is to take inventory of what is happening to him.

He understands that his sickness is related to his own sin, and he knows that God is taking his sin quite seriously, hence the demand for serious prayer and reflection.

Second Prayer: Confidence in God's Care

"O LORD, all my longing is before you; my sighing is not hidden from you" (Ps 38:9).

David says, "my longing is before you." He yearns for and desires God. Though God is aware of every loud roar of pain, frustration, and every soundless whimper of anguish, David is confident that the Lord is able to translate even his wordless expressions of distress into viable prayer requests.

Oftentimes, we think that because the Lord is disciplining us, this means He has stopped listening or has turned His back on us. But the reality is quite the opposite. The discipline of the Lord is the intimate involvement of your heavenly Father in the formation of Christlikeness in you. It's the purging of self-trust, rotten attitudes, selfishness, and complaining. The Lord is like a loving surgeon who makes a painful incision but will faithfully put you back together as well.

In his prophecy of Israel's future restoration, Isaiah mentions God's severe judgment on the Jews for their idolatry and rejection of God as the one true God. However, a promise is made: there will be a day "when the LORD binds up the brokenness of his people, and heals the wounds inflicted by his blow" (Isa 30:26).

Second Reflection: David's Complete Brokenness

My heart throbs; my strength fails me, and the light of my eyes—it also has gone from me. My friends and companions stand aloof from my plague, and my nearest kin stand far off. Those who seek my life lay their snares; those who seek my hurt speak of ruin and meditate treachery all day long. But I am like a deaf man; I do not hear, like a mute man who does not open his mouth. I have become like a man who does not hear, and in whose mouth are no rebukes (Ps 38:10-14).

David is broken *physically*, as we've already seen. He's also broken *by his friends*. Those who should be closest to him during this time are keeping their distance. It's not just because they don't want to catch whatever David has, but they "stand aloof" and "stand far off." These words both mean "to take a stand." Those closest to him are distancing themselves during his greatest time of trial. Perhaps they agree that God is disciplining David, so they want nothing to do with him and abandon him. There may not be open hostility, but there is, at the very least, a neutrality and lack of care. David is a king, and, just like anyone else in a position of power, has a difficult time knowing who his real friends are.

David is also broken *by his enemies*. His enemies lay "snares," "speak of ruin," and "meditate treachery." However, these are not the words of national enemies who are plotting to invade because they know David is sick. David's illness probably wasn't known outside his palace, which meant that those who did know were disloyal friends and family. They might see this as an opportunity to secretly plot David's downfall (38:13). We know it happened at least once when David's third son, Absalom, usurped the throne from him for a time, causing an outbreak of civil war.

Lastly, David is broken *by embarrassment*. David makes no defense, blames no one else, and gives no rebuke for another—certainly not for the Lord! He is stunned by humiliation like a deaf-mute man. He has retreated within himself, as this issue is just between him and the Lord. In his second reflection, David has come to the end of himself, completely broken and humiliated.

Third Prayer: Confidence in God's Answer

"But for you, O LORD, do I wait; it is you, O LORD my God, who will answer" (Ps 38:15).

The Lord is in charge of timing and is the source of relief. David calls God by name, "O LORD," followed by *Adonai Elohim,* meaning

"God my Master." His second prayer of verse 9 expresses a general confidence that God knows his every cry and every pain, but this is more specific. Not only does God know every cry and every pain, but He is going to do something about it.

How does David know this? The Hebrew verb "who will answer" is used as a contingent, imperfect verb which means that if certain conditions or contingencies are met, then actions will be taken. David has confidence that God will answer because certain conditions will be met. What are these conditions?

Third Reflection: Reasons God Will Answer

For I said, "Only let them not rejoice over me, who boast against me when my foot slips!" For I am ready to fall, and my pain is ever before me. I confess my iniquity; I am sorry for my sin. But my foes are vigorous, they are mighty, and many are those who hate me wrongfully. Those who render me evil for good accuse me because I follow after good (Ps 38:16-20).

David now reflects on the reasons for his confidence in God. He knows *God won't let the wicked boast forever.* "For the sake of Your faithfulness," David prays, "don't let my enemies triumph!" and God answers this prayer. Unlike most kings in the ancient world, David died in peace with his kingdom secure. He even managed to make sure that his favored son, Solomon, would ascend the throne after him.

God won't let him die in defeat. David is concerned that God's character not be tarnished. He asserted in Psalm 37 that God would establish the way of a true worshiper of God who loves the Lord and follows Him. "The steps of a man are established by the LORD, when he delights in his way; though he fall, he shall not be cast headlong, for the LORD upholds his hand" (Ps 37:23-24). But now, David says, "I am ready to fall." For the sake of *God's* name and the reputation of *God's* integrity, David believes He will keep His promise to uphold David and prevent him from final defeat.

God's forgiveness is available (38:18). Though he was troubled by guilt and the consequences of sin, David clings to the Lord with assurance of forgiveness. This is such a core truth of the gospel of Christ: God's forgiveness is available to all who ask. David was a saved man. He was a man after God's own heart. The forgiveness he sought wasn't salvation forgiveness, but a request for God to withdraw His hand of discipline from David's life.

To the unsaved, to the one who still has the burden of the debt of sin and piled-up offenses against the holiness of God, Jesus says, "Come to me, all who labor and are heavy laden, and I will give you rest" (Matt 11:28). Rest from trying to please God with your useless good works. Rest from trying to earn God's favor. Rest from wishing that God would just overlook and not see the countless ways you have violated His law, His holiness, and His character. For the saved, like David, "If we confess our sins, he is faithful and just to forgive us our sins and to cleanse us from all unrighteousness" (1 John 1:9). David knew that his illness was related to his own sinful rebellion against God, but he was also confident that forgiveness was available to him by God's grace and mercy!

God will vindicate His own (38:19-20). Even though David had sinned, he confesses his sin and believes God will restore him if for no other reason than to protect the character of His own name. The fact that David's situation was getting worse reminds him that the time for it to get better is getting closer.

David's third reflection boils down to his understanding that, "I have reasons for confidence in God, and at the top of the list is the fact that I am humbly confessing my sin before the Lord."

Final Prayer: Repeated Request for Reconciliation

"Do not forsake me, O LORD! O my God, be not far from me! Make haste to help me, O LORD, my salvation!" (Ps 38: 21-22).

Based on his humility and on the confidence he has regained, David makes one more request for reconciliation. He calls to the Lord three times and addresses God in three different ways. First, he calls to "YHWH" or "LORD"—the covenant name of God who promises to be faithful to His children. Second, he calls to "my God"—an endearing phrase like "my Father." And third, he calls to "O Lord, my salvation" as in "Master" and "Savior"—the Lord of the universe who is powerful enough to save.

David's prayer to God is, "You are Lord, and I am in covenant with You. You are a covenant-keeping God; You are my Father; You are my Master, I am Your servant. You are my Savior, the forgiver of my sins and the vindicator of Your own." The question David asks is: Can those who place their faith in the Lord pray with confidence to be delivered from severe discipline when they repent of sin? The answer he finally receives is: Yes!

There is a sense of hope from Psalm 38 that in your self-examination, as you come to the Lord in humility, he may give relief if the suffering is connected to sin. If relief is not given, you still need to pursue Christlikeness and will benefit greatly from the self-examination of your life. How do you pursue this process of self-examination? It doesn't happen through merely five minutes of reflection, but over days, weeks, and sometimes months.

The point is not to get rid of the trial, but to use your suffering as a catalyst, or incentive, for self-examination and real change. Sanctification is the work of the Holy Spirit because as we pursue Christlikeness, it is the *Holy Spirit* who produces fruit in us. We need to ask the Lord to increase the harvest of the fruit of the Spirit. Take some time to thoughtfully answer these ten questions as you examine your life for areas you need to change.

1. *Am I willing to produce a list of every specific sin I can think of?* Understand that "there is therefore now no condemnation for those who are in Christ Jesus," (Rom 8:1) but also understand that we need to "lay aside every weight, and sin which clings so closely, and let us run with endurance the race that is set before us" (Heb 12:1). David must have had a pretty good idea of what he had done because Psalm 38 seems to indicate that he was confessing specific sins to the Lord. This exercise is not for the purpose of self-condemnation, but for sanctification by

the Holy Spirit and increased awareness of which sins easily entangle you.

2. *Am I willing to add to this list the sinful thoughts I regularly harbor? How about complaints, mischaracterizations, and gossip, both in my mind and in my speech?* Replace these thoughts with "whatever is true, whatever is honorable, whatever is just, whatever is pure, whatever is lovely, whatever is commendable, if there is any excellence, if there is anything worthy of praise, think about these things" (Phil 4:8).

3. *Am I willing to add to this list those sins others point out?* Instead of being angry with your spouse, parent, brother, or sister for pointing out sin, include these additional sins on your list. This might include going back to the person(s) and asking for gentle clarification. Admit that you need to see this feedback, even if given imperfectly or even ungraciously. Think of it as a gift from the Lord to make you more like Christ.

4. *Am I willing to meditate on how I have rationalized sin?* What excuses have I made? Who have I blamed? What reasons have I given myself for looking the other way? How have I feared man and rationalized sin to please myself and others?

5. *When will I take time to confess these sins in detail to the Lord?* In Psalm 32:5, David said, "I acknowledged my sin to you, and I did not cover my iniquity; I said, 'I will confess my transgressions to the LORD,' and you forgave the iniquity of my sin." Just like David, we need to learn to come to the cool, refreshing waters of repentance instead of continually eating the sour bitterness of our own pride and self-justification.

6. *What Scriptures do I need to meditate on to help with these sins?* Do I need to go to Proverbs for the sin of laziness or sins related to anger and misuse of my tongue? Do I need to read 1 Thessalonians to help me be a better brother or sister to my fellow believers? Do I need to search the Psalms to help me repent

of not taking time to be with the Lord? Do I need to flip through Philippians to repent of great worry? Do I need reminders from Song of Solomon for how to be a loving husband or wife?

7. *How have I trusted in myself instead of the Lord? How can I practice distrusting my own wisdom?* I can't trust my emotions. I can't trust my gut reactions. I can't trust how I've always done things, but I can trust in God's Word and in God's Spirit to help me carry out His Word.

8. *On this list of specific sins, which ones are long-time patterns that need extra attention?* I need to learn that the old Adam, though mortally wounded, dies hard, so I must keep putting to death my sinful nature. "I have been crucified with Christ" (Gal 2:20).

9. *What specific actions may be required to demonstrate true repentance?* If you were making your best guess, what would be at the top of your list that you need to work on? What practical steps do you need to take in order to be more pleasing to the Lord in this area?

10. *How can I bring these issues to memory more easily?* Remember, this is not for the purpose of self-condemnation, since you are forgiven and your legal, judicial standing before the Lord is solid. Do what David did to remind himself of the Lord's kind, though tough discipline: he wrote Psalm 38 as a "memorial offering" to remember how the Lord had humbled him.

David seeks the Lord in a long period of prayer, reflection, prayer, reflection, prayer, reflection, and prayer. He approaches God not just for emotional comfort but also for understanding, growth, and renewal. If right now you're thinking, "So-and-so really needs to read this," or "Yeah, I'm pretty good in this area. I don't think this intense kind of prayer and reflection really applies to me," then examine yourself and see if you really are a regenerate believer in Christ. The true believer longs and yearns for Christlikeness and obedience because he loves the Lord. Charles Spurgeon once said:

When a man pants after God, it is a secret life within which makes him do it: he would not long after God by nature. No man thirsts for God while he is left in his carnal state. The un-renewed man pants after anything sooner than God… It proves a renewed nature when you long after God; it is a work of grace in your soul, and you may be thankful for it."[xx]

For David and for us, any trial can be viewed as an opportunity to take not a few moments, but a period of time to enter into extended prayer and reflection, to take inventory of our growth in the Lord. It is suffering which leads us to lean on Jesus Christ all the more and to demonstrate His character in our lives.

In 1820, in Dublin, Ireland, a boy named Joseph was born to a prosperous family. He learned suffering at an early age, and before he was twenty-five he was estranged from some of his family due to his Protestant faith in Christ. Joseph met a lovely young woman and became engaged, but the night before he was to be married, his beloved fiancé drowned. He immigrated to Port Hope, Canada to start his life over again as a school teacher. Years later he met a new young woman and they were engaged to be married, but she died of either pneumonia or tuberculosis just before the wedding.

Joseph's charity, his massive impact on the community, and his giving, loving Christ-like character earned him the nickname of "The Good Samaritan." When he learned that his mother back in Ireland was seriously ill, Joseph was not able to return to her, but wrote a new poem to remind her of the love of her Savior. Joseph Scriven's poem was originally called "Pray Without Ceasing," which we now know as "What a Friend We Have In Jesus."

What a friend we have in Jesus,
All our sins and griefs to bear!
What a privilege to carry
Everything to God in prayer!
Oh, what peace we often forfeit,
Oh, what needless pain we bear,

All because we do not carry
Everything to God in prayer!

Have we trials and temptations?
Is there trouble anywhere?
We should never be discouraged;
Take it to the Lord in prayer.
Can we find a friend so faithful
Who will all our sorrows share?
Jesus knows our every weakness,
Take it to the Lord in prayer.

Are we weak and heavy-laden,
Cumbered with a load of care?
Precious Savior, still our refuge;
Take it to the Lord in prayer.
Do thy friends despise, forsake thee?
Take it to the Lord in prayer.
In His arms He'll take and shield thee;
Thou wilt find a solace there.

13

Eve Says, "Humbly Forgive Those Who Have Caused Sorrow"

If we made a list of the most heinous and atrocious sinners of all time, who might come to mind? Certainly, Judas has to be near the top. Jesus called him the son of destruction. Judas betrayed the very Son of God, and we know that he did not repent of his deeds (John 17:12). Another candidate might be the apostle Paul, who called himself the foremost of sinners (1 Tim 1:15). Paul had persecuted the church and had been present at the death of the first Christian martyr, Stephen. Later, Christ miraculously saved Paul by His grace and used him mightily for the kingdom of God.

There have been many men in history responsible for horrific crimes against humanity and the deaths of thousands and even millions. But only one man in history can claim the dubious distinction of being responsible for the deaths of 100 billion people and counting. First Corinthians tells us that because of Adam, the representation of humanity, all die. God created Adam and placed him in a garden in the land of Eden with one restriction:

The LORD God took the man and put him in the Garden of Eden to work it and keep it. And the LORD God commanded the man, saying, "You may surely eat of every tree of the garden, but of the tree of the knowledge of good and evil you shall not eat, for in the day that you eat of it, you shall surely die" (Gen 2:15-17).

This command was given before God created a woman for Adam, so he was the responsible party for transferring God's words to his wife and family. Soon after, God created the best thing he had ever made: a woman. But Eve, as she was later named, succumbed to the temptation to disobey the Lord. Satan himself, in the form of a serpent, tempted her to eat of the tree of the knowledge of good and evil.

Adam and Eve had known of the possibility of evil, but now they had the experiential knowledge of what it meant to rebel against the God who had created and loved them. Genesis 3:7 says that their eyes were opened. They had enjoyed a world with the complete freedom of absolute sinlessness, not even being constrained by clothing! But a huge shift occurred because of this choice, and Adam and Eve were now physically and spiritually naked and ashamed and hid themselves from the presence of God.

Even though the woman ate the forbidden fruit first, God held Adam responsible. Romans 5:12 confirms this saying, "sin came into the world through one man." Theologians call this the federal headship of Adam. Why Adam and not Eve? While the complex answer to that question is beyond the span of this chapter, suffice to say that the inspired revelation of the New Testament confirms Adam's ultimate responsibility before God.

Scripture demonstrates God's grace extended to Adam and Eve in that God offered them salvation. First, although he had sinned and knew he deserved death, Adam didn't immediately die. In fact, he was given the grace of almost 1,000 years of life! Second, God gave Adam and Eve a temporary covering for their sin through the shedding of blood, "And the LORD God made for Adam and for his wife garments of skins and clothed them" (Gen 3:21).

It would be strange to use this picture of substitution if Adam and Eve were to be eternally punished for their sin. Genesis 4:26 indicates that Adam was among those who "began to call upon the name of the LORD." Adam and Eve were also given the hope of a Savior through the first prophecy of the Messiah: "I will put enmity between you and the woman, and between your offspring and her offspring; he shall bruise your head, and you shall bruise his heel" (3:15).

Future salvation aside, Eve took the first bite, but Adam was the one held responsible by God for the entrance of sin and death into the world. We are not told what would have happened to Eve if Adam had refused to eat, but in the sovereign plan of God, Adam chose to take the fruit. The fact is, God held Adam accountable.

This is not to say that Eve was off the hook. Because of her choice to disobey God, she experienced personal consequences that would also extend to all women: pain in the child-bearing process, anguish of bringing children into the world who would disappoint their parents with their own sin and eventually die, and the loss of the natural tendency to be a loving helper to her husband.

Suffering is not always at the hands of inanimate objects like cancer cells or unfeeling entities such as Corporate America, which gives and takes jobs at a whim without thought of the devastation that comes to a family. Very often, our suffering comes at the hands of someone close to us who has deeply hurt and shocked us. The sense of betrayal and anguish is profound, and the feeling of duplicity, treachery, and disappointment is so staggering that many people say they would rather endure any other trial than a relationship trial.

To make it worse, this trial may be ongoing—a husband or wife who hurts you deeply, a child who has rejected and abandoned his relationship with you, or a fellow believer or church member who has wounded you in a way you never expected. The hardest part of a trial involving another person is the inability to forgive and move on.

We have a difficult time letting God be God. We need to stop thinking of the other person as less worthy of God's affection than us, stop wishing for their downfall, stop desiring hell and damnation on those who have hurt us, and stop waiting for someone to be perfected before we decide they are worthy of our forgiveness.

What Eve Lost Because of Adam

At the outset, let me say that we could just as easily write "what Adam lost because of Eve." Both ate the fruit in rebellion to God's will; both fell. Both needed God's forgiveness and the mutual forgiveness of one another. Both lost almost everything. But I have chosen to focus on Eve because she, as a wife counting on her husband, suffered so very much. She lost a righteous and attentive husband, a luxurious home in Eden, direct access to God, and ultimately her life, but through all this she still humbly forgave Adam and loved him to the end.

Eve Lost a Righteous Husband

Before Adam allowed himself to be persuaded to sin, he had been perfectly kind and perfectly loving. He had been the perfect best friend to Eve, and their companionship was sweet and always fresh and delightful. But now, that original Adam was gone, replaced by a sinful version of the man Eve once knew. Adam's natural tendency would no longer be toward kindness and gentleness. Instead, it would be to dominate and lord over his wife. All married women understand, to some degree, Eve's disappointment. On your wedding day you thought you knew who you were marrying, but after a few years you think, "This isn't the man I married!"

For married women today, what they lose is a fantasy—the make-believe illusion of a perfect husband. Eve, however, really *did* lose the perfect husband! We don't know how long Eve lived, but we do know that Adam was 130 years old when Eve bore Seth. Adam lived for another 800 years, so Eve could have been married to him for 800 or 900 years. Talk about having a long memory for sin!

Eve Lost an Attentive Husband

When Adam was first created, he enjoyed the pleasure of sin-free, reasonably easy work, tending the Garden of Eden. But with the entrance of sin,

Adam would have to toil and sweat from sunup to sundown just to put food on the table to survive. Now he had to work to the point of exhaustion for each meal, fighting thorns, weeds, and difficult manual labor. Not only had Eve lost a righteous husband, but she had also lost an attentive husband. She would be given the leftovers of Adam's energy as he ended each day shattered, drained, and grunting his way through an evening meal. She got a smelly, sweaty, exhausted, frustrated man desperately trying to squeeze a living out of uncooperative land.

Ladies, some of you are weeping inside right now because you understand this. Your husbands are living under the same curse as Adam. Many wives have used the phrase, "I remember when we used to go on dates, spend more time together, and not have children underfoot all the time."

But no wife ever had it as bad as Eve. What wife could ever say, "I remember when we used to take relaxing, glorious walks for days at a time in a perfect garden in the perfect land of Eden, talking and enjoying one another—and we didn't even have to wear clothes! Remember when our marriage was one long, lovely honeymoon?" Eve would be the first of countless wives to try to get the attention of her tired husband.

Eve Lost Her Home

There have been many theories for the location of the Garden of Eden, the place of "delightful luxury."[xxi] When Christopher Columbus passed the exit point of the Orinoco River in South America, he assumed the waters came from Eden. In the 19th century, one popular author theorized that the rivers from Eden flowed from the North Pole. British general, Charles George Gordon, believed after his world travels that Eden was located on a beautiful island in the Indian Ocean.

But Moses, author of the book of Genesis, tells us simply that Adam and Eve's home was "in Eden, in the east" (Gen 2:8). From Moses' perspective, either from Mount Sinai or from the plains of Moab, the country of Eden would have been east. The best guess for the garden, then, would probably be in Mesopotamia near the Persian Gulf.

Genesis 2:9 describes this beautiful garden as having "every tree that is pleasant to the sight and good for food." This is amazing, considering there are an estimated 23,000 different kinds of trees in the world, as a conservative estimate. There is something majestic, comforting, and regal about trees. They are artistically designed by God to draw the eye upward, to continually point your line of vision toward the heavens. Adam and Eve would have enjoyed almonds, apples, apricots, avocados, cherries, coconuts, oranges, lemons, limes, grapefruit, figs, guavas, peaches, pears, pecans, persimmons, plums, and olives, just to name a few! And this didn't even include berry bushes, shrubs, and other edible plants.

The garden included the "tree of life," which in some way was God's means to preserve life. We're not told how, but we do know that the tree of life will appear once again in the New Jerusalem as described at the end of Revelation. Another significant tree was the "tree of the knowledge of good and evil," designed by God for Adam to worship Him by demonstrating obedience to His command.

Rivers flowing from a subterranean source watered the immense land of Eden. A better translation of the "mist" in Genesis 2:6 is a "stream" or "fountain" that watered the land. Some people suggest that the four rivers mentioned in Genesis 2:10-14 actually flowed *into* Eden, forming one large river that watered the land, but there is more support for the river of Eden being the source river.[xxii] The Tigris and Euphrates have been located today, but the source of the Pishon and Gihon are still unknown. Undoubtedly, Noah's descendants carried the cultural memory (and perhaps even written records) of these four rivers after the catastrophic flood. Finding two rivers where there used to be four, it would be natural to rename them using the pre-flood names with which they were familiar.

The theological significance of Eden gives us a clue about the direction the rivers flowed: they flowed outward. The Garden of Eden was the first-ever sanctuary of God. It was where Adam and Eve could worship Him, it was the location of the tree of life and the tree of the knowledge of good and evil, and it was where Adam and Eve met with God face to face in a theophany, or physical manifestation of God. The sanctuary of God, the place to meet God, is often associated with a mountain (Mt. Sinai, the Mount of Transfiguration, the holy mountain of God in Psalm 48, etc.). If the rivers flowed *out*, then the Garden of Eden was likely at the top of a mountain from which the whole country of Eden was watered and from where Adam and Eve could survey the land. Since Adam was the co-regent king of the earth who was appointed to rule, it would make sense that he ruled from a mountaintop (Gen 1:28).

> Now out of the ground the LORD God had formed every beast of the field and every bird of the heavens and brought them to the man to see what he would call them. And whatever the man called every living creature, that was its name. The man gave names to all livestock and to the birds of the heavens and to every beast of the field (Gen 2:19-20a).

Adam enjoyed an entire zoo that adored him as their ruler. Because of the curse, a healthy distance has been kept between mankind and animals, but this was not so in Eden. Animals were a blessing; they were intelligent and responded to the names that Adam gave them. What a home Eve had—a mountaintop garden with rivers, expanses, trees, and friendly birds and animals of every kind—and she was the queen of it all.

But... Adam lost it all! "Then the LORD God said, 'Behold, the man has become like one of us in knowing good and evil. Now, lest he reach out his hand and take also of the tree of life and eat, and live forever'" (Gen 3:22). Adam sought autonomy from God. He wanted to decide for himself what was right and wrong instead of following God. In this, he had become like God and was trying to become sovereign, but this resulted in disaster as Adam tried to escape the Lordship of God. So God gave him over to his choice, and Adam chose evil.

God was actually gracious to not allow Adam to live forever in a sinful state. So although He kept him from the tree of life, the consequences of this situation were catastrophic for Adam and Eve, and they lost their beloved home.

> Therefore the LORD God sent him out from the Garden of Eden to work the ground from which he was taken. He drove out the man, and at the east of the Garden of Eden he placed the cherubim and a flaming sword that turned every way to guard the way to the tree of life (Gen 3:23-24).

As Adam and Eve walked out of the Garden, Eve may have looked back at her cherished home and seen the guard that God had placed at the entrance. It would be impossible for Adam to say "I'm sorry" enough times to make up for this devastating loss. Not only did Eve lose a righteous husband and an attentive husband, but she lost the only home she had ever known.

Eve Lost Direct Access to God

> And they heard the sound of the LORD God walking in the garden in the cool of the day, and the man and his wife hid themselves from the presence of the LORD God among the trees of the garden. But the LORD God called to the man and said to him, "Where are you?" And he said, "I heard the sound of you in the garden, and I was afraid, because I was naked, and I hid myself" (Gen 3:8-10).

Since Adam and his wife were hiding from God, this implied that they had previously enjoyed complete, direct access to God. The Garden of Eden was God's chosen dwelling place among men. There was no curtain of separation; the Garden of Eden was the original Holy of Holies, the inner dwelling place of God where Adam and Eve walked with God in peace and perfect fellowship and communion.

The garden was a sacred space devoted to perfect companionship with God. In describing the future temple of God, Moses wrote in Deuteronomy 12 that the temple would be the "dwelling place of God," the place where men would meet with God. But until Christ's ultimate sacrifice, Jews would meet with Him only on the basis of bringing a blood sacrifice to atone for their sins. Adam and Eve had been given a great privilege to meet with God.

Perhaps the closest idea we have to understanding what Eve went through in her loss is the loss the disciples experienced when Jesus went away to heaven. They were so distraught over His upcoming departure that Jesus used five whole chapters in John to comfort and reassure them (John 13-17). Eve had enjoyed sweet, uninterrupted friendship with her

Maker, Almighty God, but her last memory of Him in the garden was watching Him slaughter an animal to cover her sin. God provided a temporary substitute for Adam and Eve, who should have died for their rebellion, but He also drove Eve and her husband away from His holy place, away from His direct presence.

The loss of perfect fellowship with God can't be estimated in value. We've never seen God face to face. We've never walked with Him in the sweetness of the Garden of Eden. Adam and Eve would have to exercise something for the first time, something that is now so familiar to us: faith. They now had to walk in sightless faith. They had once enjoyed God at a close range, but He now stood aloof from them in His holiness. Eve's relationship with God was reduced to something distant, something that would need a Mediator someday.

Eve Lost Her Life

Worst of all, Eve lost her life. "By the sweat of your face you shall eat bread, till you return to the ground, for out of it you were taken; for you are dust, and to dust you shall return" (Gen 3:19). There would be a day when the curse of sin would finally catch up to her, and her body would weaken, her vitality would drain, and her age would make her suffer until she succumbed to a final breath and a final heartbeat. Death is not a wonderful, natural cycle—it is a horrifying result of Adam's rebellion against God as the representative of humanity. It is possible that Adam was still alive when Eve died. Imagine how close they would have become after living together for centuries. Now she was gone, and it was all his fault.

As Eve continued to age, she experienced the consequences of all the losses we've just listed. With the astonishing amount of loss she endured, Eve could be categorized as one who walked through a terrible river of suffering, and she could personally point to the one man whom God deemed responsible, yet Eve did something incredibly godly: she forgave Adam.

After all, it was because of Adam that she had lost her perfect marriage, the complete attention of her husband, her home in Eden, sweet communion with God, and ultimately her battle with whatever disease finally killed her. Nevertheless, *she forgave Adam.*

Evidence that Eve Forgive Adam

How do we know that Eve truly forgave Adam? We see three lines of evidence through her relationship with the Lord, her reliability with Adam, and her recognition of her personal sin.

Eve's Relationship with the Lord

We can't imagine loss of this magnitude, yet Eve continued on in faithfulness to the Lord. "Now Adam knew Eve his wife, and she conceived and bore Cain, saying, 'I have gotten a man with the help of the LORD'" (Gen 4:1). There are some significant translation questions in this verse. In Hebrew it reads, "I have acquired [or created] a man with the LORD." There is evidence that Eve believed this was the promised Messiah of Genesis 3:15, since this verse is possible to translate as, "I have gotten a man, the LORD."

This is a debate for another day, but in any case, the Lord God alone is credited with giving Eve a son. Eve acknowledged God's care and sovereignty in her life through her baby boy. Notice how these are not the words of a bitter woman, but of a believer and worshiper of God who is in a right relationship with Him. She expressed humble thankfulness to God for blessing her so much.

What is the connection between forgiving Adam and being thankful for her son? Eve had received and accepted the Lord's help, and she was content with her situation and grateful for the blessings she now possessed. You cannot be in right relationship with the Lord while in the midst of bitterness and unforgiveness. After the tragedy of their son Cain growing up to murder their second son Abel, God provided Adam and Eve with another son, Seth, as a replacement for Abel. Once again, Eve expressed her heartfelt gratitude to the Lord, "And Adam knew his wife again, and she bore a son and called his name Seth, for she said, 'God has appointed for me another offspring instead of Abel, for Cain killed him'" (Gen 4:25). This is not the disposition of a sour, nasty, unpleasant, acrimonious woman, but of a woman at peace with her God and her circumstances and, by inference, her husband.

Eve's Reliability with Adam

Today, the majority of divorces are initiated by women. Studies range from just over 50% to 75%, but there seems to be a general agreement that women initiate divorce more than men do. Couples over the age of forty-five are now divorcing at a much higher rate than they were even a decade ago, with one author citing a 30% increase[xxiii]. The most common reason given for divorce has been marital infidelity, but that is quickly losing the battle for the new number one reason. There is a growing phenomenon among women to leave their husbands for a more exciting life. In 2011, Julia Llewellyn Smith wrote about this trend in an article called "Women and Divorce: Goodbye, Darling, You're Just Too Dull."[xxiv] Citing a survey of family attorneys, she stated that more and more women say they are leaving their husbands because they're bored. This is complete, total narcissism.

As Christians, we understand that God hates divorce because we understand the sanctity of marriage. From a purely human standpoint, if any woman had the right to say, "I'm done," it would surely have been Eve. Obviously, our first question is, "Where else would she go? How would she live?" Countless men and women have left their spouses without answers to these questions. All speculation aside, she persevered through life with Adam—the man who was legally, before God, responsible for her current plight. All the way to Genesis 5:5, which records the death of Adam, we see nothing but a unified Adam and Eve together.

Here's one more clue that Eve lived in peace with Adam. Adam was the appointed co-regent king of the earth; he named all the animals according to their character (Gen 4:1, 25). After the Fall, he also named his wife, "Eve," which meant "mother of all living." But Adam gave Eve the privilege and joy of naming the children. Eve, though her life was radically altered by her husband's lack of leadership and godly example, apparently worked at endearing herself to him. She loved him, and he in return loved her.

Eve's Recognition of Personal Sin

Perhaps the most compelling evidence for why Eve forgave Adam was the awareness of her own sin, a keen understanding that is unique in all of history. She not only gave birth to children in great physical pain, but she raised these sinful children, one of whom would be a murderer. Eve felt first-hand the results of God's decree that He would multiply her pain in childbearing, and in pain she would bring forth children (Gen 3:16). She and Adam stand alone as the only humans in history who were sinners but remembered what it was like not to sin. She could see that her new desire was to lash out and usurp her husband. She had sinned against God, and yet in His mercy she still lived. God's mediated forgiveness was available to her through bloodshed, as we've already seen.

Based on the grace that Eve had received, she extended this same grace to Adam. After all, although he was held responsible, she ate the fruit, too. She rebelled against God just as Adam did, and God had been merciful to her just as he was to Adam. When your trial offers you the opportunity to forgive, you must. It's a command of God, and, in fact, to decide not to forgive can indicate that you are not a regenerate, true believer in Christ.

Many ask, "What if the person who offended me has not repented or acknowledged their wrong?" We are still commanded to have the attitude of forgiveness. The relationship may be strained or difficult, but there should be no sense in which you view the other person as unforgivable or unworthy of forgiveness. If repentance happens, the attitude of forgiveness can include a full restoration of the relationship.

Decisions of a Forgiving Heart

Forgiveness involves a series of decisions. I'll highlight just six of them:

1. *"I will not keep an active, cumulative record of wrongs."* Isaiah 43:35 says that the Lord keeps no record of wrongs of those He has forgiven, so you, too, can forgive individual offenses. More often than not, our sinful tendency is to accumulate offenses

that cause us to make a broad, global judgment about someone, placing them in an unforgiveable position. A wife might tell her husband, "You are a rude, insensitive jerk!" How is he supposed to repent of that? However, if she said, "Yesterday, you treated me badly with your words," then the heart issue can be addressed.

2. *"I will not let my emotions lead the way."* Forgiveness has nothing to do with emotion and everything to do with obedience. In Luke 17 Jesus used the analogy of an obedient slave doing that which he didn't *feel* like doing to communicate our duty to forgive.

3. *"I will cancel the debt that is owed to me."* Sin creates indebtedness. This is why our sinful urge of vengeance demands to be fully repaid that which we think is owed to us. God is clear in Scripture that vengeance is His alone to take (Heb 10:30). When someone hurts or offends you, and you immediately add that to your growing list of all the other times that he or she has done the same crime, it becomes bitterness. You are continuing to withhold the forgiveness of that debt.

4. *"I will not entertain thoughts of this offense anymore."* Bitterness is an internal sin that manifests itself externally. It is the cause of all verbal and physical violence between those who profess to love each other. And it all starts in the mind, cultivating thoughts of self-evaluation and entitlement, and judging another person as undeserving of forgiveness while viewing yourself as deserving.

5. *"I will not use this offense against the offender in my thoughts, conversations, or actions."* This falls in line with the fact that, judicially, God will never hold your sin against you. He will certainly discipline disobedience because there are natural consequences to sin, but He will never judge you as guilty anymore.

6. *"I will listen to the one who has offended me to see how I might improve in my sanctification."* Rarely do offenses happen in a

vacuum; they happen in relationships. Much growth can come from the humility of listening to someone who has injured you and being attentive to their perspective.

These are difficult truths to swallow, but they're true. With many trials in life, you have no control over how much pain you are in, but with people who have caused you sorrow, you have all the tools necessary to stop suffering. The answer is: forgive them. How did Jesus forgive? He told a paralyzed man, "Son, your sins are forgiven." That's it? That's it!

The lesson from Eve is clear. By becoming deeply aware of our own sin and the grace that God has shown us, there is no offense too great to forgive. Eve lost her home, and in order to provide forgiveness, Christ lost His heavenly home for a time to come to earth. Eve lost direct access to God, and Christ lost direct access to His Father for a time, being reduced to mere prayer instead of the direct, sweet communion of eternity past. Eve lost her life, and Christ lost His life to pay for her sin, for Adam's sin, and for the sin of the one who has offended you.

Eve forgave Adam. Christ forgave Adam. Christ forgave you. How could you do any less, when you have lost so little in comparison?

14

Heman Says,
"Be Confident in the Lord's Presence
in the Darkness"

God calls us to truly comfort, encourage, and serve one another. We come as the flesh-and-blood presence of God to those experiencing the deep isolation that suffering often brings. But distressingly, we can fail others and others likewise fail us. When we are suffering, our loneliness and emotional or physical seclusion can be easily overlooked or forgotten by others.

In 1872 Jane Ellice Hopkins published a book entitled *Christ the Consoler: A Book of Comfort for the Sick.* Sensing that the sick often received more advice than comfort, Jane wanted to write something that said, "Someone else understands!" The following selection from Jane's book provides insight for our next character's lesson.

"There are times when an unspeakable sadness steals upon me, an immense loneliness takes possession of my soul, a longing perchance for some vanished hand and voice to comfort me as of old, a desolation without form and void, that wraps me in its folds, and darkens my inmost being. It was not thus in the first days of my illness.

"Then all was so new and strange, that a strange spiritual strength filled my soul, and seemed to bear me up as with angel hands. The love and kindness that my sickness called forth, came to me with a sweet surprise; tender solicitude made my very pain into an occasion of joy to me; and hope was strong and recovery was near, only a few brief weeks between me and returning health, with nothing of sickness remaining, but the memory of all that love and sympathy, like a line of light my Saviour's feet had left, as He walked with me on the troubled sea.

"But now that hope is deferred, and returning health seems to loiter by the way, and recovery is delayed, and the trial lengthens out like an ever lengthening chain, my soul begins to faint and tire, and the burden to grow heavier. Even to those who love me most, my pain and helplessness is now an accustomed thing, while to me it keeps its keen edge of suffering, but little dulled by use.

"My ills to them are a tedious oft told tale which comes with something of a dull reiterance. It has become almost a matter of course that in the pleasant plan I should be left out, that in the pleasant walk I should be left behind; a matter of course that the pleasures of life should pass me by with folded hand and averted face; and sickness, and monotonous days, and grey shadows should be my portion…

"And O my God, my spirit sometimes faints beneath a nameless dread that this loneliness will grow deeper and deeper, if it be Thy will that my sickness should continue, or recovery be long delayed. I can no longer be the companion of those I love; shall I be as dear to them as if I could have kept by their side, and been bound up with all their active interests and pleasures? I have to see others take my place, and do my work for them; shall I not suffer loss in their eyes, and others enter into the heritage of love which might have been mine?

"Will they not grow weary of me, weary of the same old ills, oft repeated, but ever new, and turn with an unconscious feeling of relief, to brighter hearts, and more joyous lives?

"My God, my God, to whom can I turn for comfort but unto Thee, Thou who didst drink the bitter cup of human loneliness to the dregs that Thou mightiest make Thyself a brother to the lonely, a merciful and faithful High Priest to the desolate soul; Thou who alone canst pass within, the doors being *shut to all human aid, into that secret place of thunder, where the tempest tossed soul suffers and struggles alone; Thou who alone canst command the winds and tempests, and say unto the sea "Be still!" and unto the wind, "Blow not!" and there shall be a great calm. As a child alone in the dark, my heart cries out for Thee, cries for Thine embracing arms, for Thy voice of comfort, for Thy pierced heart on which to rest my aching head, and feel that Love is near."*

Jane spoke of her family and friends getting tired of hearing about her malady. She spoke of being left out of activities. She spoke of being replaced by others in her duties. Her essay ends with the prayer, "As a child alone in the dark, my heart cries for Thee, cries for Thine embracing arms, for Thy voice of comfort." In other words, her sickness felt like an immense darkness, and she understood that the sick person needed to be confident in the Lord's presence in the midst of darkness.

Heman would have understood Jane's heart. He wrote Psalm 88 from his experience with great illness, similar to David in Psalm 38. Unlike David, Heman's theme is not his sin and repentance, but simply the darkness he feels. Heman's advice is, "Be confident in the Lord's presence in the darkness."

The Saddest Psalm

Many psalms and prayers in the Bible, such as Psalm 7 and 77, begin with lament or complaint and end with hope and victory. But Psalm 88 has no glorious ending and is sometimes referred to as the saddest Psalm. It begins and ends in seeming hopelessness. It is not on behalf of Israel, but an individual lament about one man and his interaction with God in the midst of hopelessness.

Psalm 88 is both sad and serious, but with further study we will also see the hope, faith, and strength contained in it, with the wonderful assurance that even in darkness the Lord is present and active. Ultimately, we'll see that pain and trials lead to a higher view of God, to prayer, and to an exaltation of the sovereignty of God. Even when your pain is so severe and the fire of the trial so intense that the very core of your faith is tested to its breaking point, even here, God is purifying your faith and your view of His sovereign plan and exalted character.

The author of Psalm 88 is Heman. There are several theories about Heman's identity, but not much information is known about the details of his life. The first possibility is that Heman is the poet from 1 Chronicles 6:18. His name is listed as one of the leaders of the Levites appointed by David to sing and play music in the house of God. He was the son of Joel and grandson of Samuel the prophet. The second option for his identity is in 1 Kings 4:31, "For [Solomon] was wiser than all other men, wiser than Ethan the Ezrahite, and Heman, Calcol, and Darda, the sons of Mahol." In either case, Heman was a wise worshipper of God. Undoubtedly, the many elements of Heman's suffering contributed to his wisdom.

Heman's Desperation

"O LORD, God of my salvation; I cry out day and night before you. Let my prayer come before you; incline your ear to my cry… Every day I call upon you, O LORD; I spread out my hands to you" (Ps 88: 1-2, 9).

Most agree that Heman had some type of serious terminal illness. This is the only "prayer for the sick" psalm that does not include a complaint against one's enemies, so his sickness was most likely a physical illness of some kind. It could have been an illness from his youth or something contracted in later years, but whatever it was we know that it cut him off from society. Heman's life was a living death, and his troubles were due to God's displeasure, yet he appealed to God for help. His suffering was lengthy, isolating and debilitating.

This situation was so dire that Heman cries and shouts for help. "I cry before you" is a past tense verb form with a present tense, meaning, "I have cried out to you and I continue to cry out to you!" He emphasizes his cry "before you" with the desire for his prayer to be heard. Verse 2 has two requests, and it is clear that Heman believes death is imminent. He uses dark, deathly images like the place of the dead, the underworld, and the nature of the dead. Hopelessness and desperation permeate the psalm, and there are no direct requests to be rescued. It ends with a complaint, which is highly unusual in the Psalms.

Heman's attitude of prayer comes out of desperation, not out of a structured quiet-time routine. He is asking for mercy just to be heard.

He is begging for all hindrances to be removed and for the prayer to go straight to the heart of God. He is also persistent in his prayer, "My eye grows dim through sorrow. Every day I call upon you, O LORD; I spread out my hands to you" (88:9). The "eye" refers to both eyes and can refer to loss of sight or great weeping.

Heman could be experiencing a kind of illness involving specific pain in the eyes or loss of strength. His illness is met with constant prayer, daily humility, and pleas for mercy with outspread hands. As a little child stretches out her hands to her mother while she cries, so does this afflicted child of God. Heman prays continually, his eyes weep, his voice sobs, his hands stretch heavenward, and his heart breaks. Heman's was a prayer of desperation.

Heman's Affliction

> For my soul is full of troubles, and my life draws near to Sheol. I am counted among those who go down to the pit; I am a man who has no strength, like one set loose among the dead, like the slain that lie in the grave, like those whom you remember no more, for they are cut off from your hand. You have put me in the depths of the pit, in the regions dark and deep. Your wrath lies heavy upon me, and you overwhelm me with all your waves (Ps 88:3-7).

Heman is exhausted, spiritually downcast, and possibly close to death. He can't take any more—he is full to the brim with agony. He speaks of his "soul," which can also mean "mouth" or "throat." This is a picture of being so full of troubles that he is sick. He feels like he is counted as dead (88:4). "Like the slain" is reminiscent of a wounded soldier left for dead among the slain of a bloody battlefield (88:5). The "pit" is something deep, foul, unclean, fearful, slimy, and hopeless. Heman expresses feeling forsaken by God, like a ship overwhelmed by waves to the point of sinking, with the waves crashing over him (88:7).

Nine times Heman attributes his illness to God, just as Jeremiah lamented, "Who has spoken and it came to pass, unless the LORD has commanded it? Is it not from the mouth of the Most High that good and bad come?" (Lam 3:37-38). Or as Job chided, "But he said to her, 'You speak as one of the foolish women would speak. Shall we receive good from God, and shall we not receive evil?' In all this Job did not sin with his lips" (Job 2:10). Heman feels great pressure from God in this trial, and he suspects that God may be punishing him (Ps 88:7). He's devastated that the Lord has afflicted him, he feels treated like the wicked, and he doesn't understand God's rationale.

Heman's Rejection

Heman laments that he is rejected by his loved ones. "You have caused my companions to shun me; you have made me a horror to them. I am shut in so that I cannot escape... You have caused my beloved and my friend to shun me; my companions have become darkness" (88:8, 18). Heman could have been ceremonially unclean or contagious, similar to a leper, and he felt his loneliness during this time.

According to the law, he could have been ostracized from society. Old Testament law stated, "If the man who is unclean does not cleanse himself, that person shall be cut off from the midst of the assembly, since he has defiled the sanctuary of the LORD" (Num 19:20a). Either way, *what he needed most was the companionship of friends and family.* He was rejected by his "beloved" which can be translated "lover" and "friend." Likely, his family and friends had all left him. Perhaps even his own wife had to distance herself because of his illness. He was "shut in," or literally "imprisoned," in his own body of illness or in his own house due to this contagious sickness.

This is huge. When in agony, we *need* the companionship and comfort of those closest to us. But for Heman the Lord in His sovereign wisdom didn't allow even this. If ever a time to need companionship, it was now! Heman could rely on no one else but God Himself to provide comfort.

In his physical illness that caused great pain, great weeping, and great suffering, Heman knew that God had done this and that no one else could rescue him. He felt treated like a wicked man, imprisoned by his illness, with no family or friends, utterly alone.

Heman's Disorientation

Confused, alone, and sad, Heman asks God six questions about his suffering:

> Do you work wonders for the dead? Do the departed rise up to praise you? Is your steadfast love declared in the grave, or your faithfulness in Abaddon? Are your wonders known in the darkness, or your righteousness in the land of forgetfulness? But I, O LORD, cry to you; in the morning my prayer comes before you. O LORD, why do you cast my soul away? Why do you hide Your face from me? (Ps 88:10-14).

Heman asks God, "How can I glorify God if I am dead?" Feeling abandoned and betrayed by God, Heman is distraught over the loss of communion with God. He pleads, "I'm not dead yet—I'm still alive! I can still serve you—don't give up on me!" Jews tended to focus not so much on life after death, but on their relationship with God through the Abrahamic and Davidic Covenants. The covenant blessings, in the view of the Jew, were meant to be enjoyed in life. God is a God of the living, not the dead, and the command to praise God is given to those who are alive. "The living, the living, he thanks you, as I do this day; the father makes known to the children your faithfulness" (Isa 38:19). Without New Testament revelation, they had an incomplete eschatology, but still understood these basic truths.

Heman's prayer heightens as he makes requests to God through these questions. He says, "Don't abandon me yet! I can still be useful to You!" This is the cry of someone who has experienced communion, worship, and intimacy with God and who now feels betrayed by the only one in whom he trusted.

Even the children of God's love can sometimes feel like the recipients of God's wrath. And this feeling that God may be against you can stand as the most debilitating aspect of suffering.

Heman's Desolation

"Afflicted and close to death from my youth up, I suffer your terrors; I am helpless. Your wrath has swept over me; your dreadful assaults destroy me. They surround me like a flood all day long; they close in on me together" (Ps 88:15-17). At this point, Heman surrenders. "I've been sick off and on since I was a youth, close to death numerous times. You have swept over me. You've assaulted me. I've been flooded by Your attacks against me. I am overcome. *You win!*" There is nothing he can do. He feels that God is trying to destroy him. He is completely desperate, afflicted, rejected, disoriented, and desolate.

In Anthony Scioli and Henry Biller's book, *Hope in the Age of Anxiety*, published in 2009, hopelessness is categorized into nine classifications.[xxv] Their answer to hopelessness is to restructure your thoughts and to mentally and emotionally pull yourself up by your own bootstraps. The categories of hopelessness Scioli and Biller have identified are interesting.

1. *Alienation*: Feeling you are no longer worthy of love or care

2. *Forsakenness*: Experiencing abandonment in time of need

3. *Uninspired*: Feeling like there are no more options to choose from

4. *Powerlessness*: Thinking you are completely unable to change the situation

5. *Oppression*: Feeling subjugated and down-trodden by a more powerful entity

6. *Limitedness*: Lacking the skills necessary to make the situation better

7. *Doom*: Believing death is imminent and that life is nearly over

8. *Captivity*: Feeling imprisoned by your situation

9. *Helplessness*: Feeling exposed and vulnerable; no longer thinking you can live safely in the world

According to Scioli and Biller, the cure to hopelessness is to fight it off with new thinking and new relationships and "summon the light back into our lives."[xxvi] If Heman were to take their advice, he would have been experiencing and battling all nine categories!

1. *Alienation:* "You have made me a horror to [my companions]" (88:8).

2. *Forsakenness:* "You have caused my beloved and my friend to shun me" (88:18).

3. *Uninspired (with no more options to choose from):* "Your dreadful assaults destroy me" (88:16).

4. *Powerlessness:* "I am a man who has no strength" (88:4).

5. *Oppression:* "You have put me in the depths of the pit" (88:6).

6. *Limitedness (unable to overcome the situation in his own power):* "Your dreadful assaults... close in on me together" (88:16-17).

7. *Doom:* "Afflicted and close to death" (88:15).

8. *Captivity:* "I am shut in so that I cannot escape" (88:8).

9. *Helplessness:* "I am helpless" (88:15).

Heman is suffering from every kind of hopelessness. From the world's standpoint, his response should be, "Think differently and pull yourself up." But how can he? His conclusion in verse 18 has been, "my companions have become darkness," meaning, "My only friend is darkness—it's the only companion I have!"

If you were to close this book right now, you might leave feeling the same way, but the greatest treasures are often buried in darkness. Heman felt alone, with darkness as his only companion, but through his psalm we can be confident of the Lord's presence even in the darkness.

Seven Reasons We Can Be Confident in the Lord's Presence in Darkness

First, *strength comes from God*. When pain seems to have no purpose, our faith is strengthened. Heman didn't have all the information yet; he didn't know why he had struggled with illness since he was young. He didn't know why God seemed to be oppressing him. But there is always a purpose, always a God-ordained outcome of strengthened faith. James 1:3 says that "the testing of your faith produces steadfastness."

Second, *we can experience intimacy with God*. Heman is in a place of total dependence upon God, a place where his faith is purest. There are no earthly remedies that work, no human relationships he can rely upon. It is Heman, his trial, and God—no other players in this drama. All other comforts have been refined away until Heman is facing his God. We should prefer to look face to face with God, even if it means being in the worst trial of our life, rather than be complacent and forgetful of His glory in the midst of comfort and ease.

Third, *we can trust in God*. Note how the psalm begins by calling the Lord's name: "O LORD, God of my salvation" (88:1). He acknowledges that only God can save him, and only God will receive the glory. This expresses a steadfast faith in the Lord despite His silent response. God may be the source of the pain, but He is certainly the only source of salvation.

Fourth, *we can communicate with God*. This trial has driven Heman to persistence in prayer. Heman wrestles with God through questions. He isn't afraid to engage God and doesn't appear to indict God of doing anything wrong; instead, he just wants to know that his suffering has a purpose. Heman persists in prayer precisely because he has not yet been delivered from his immediate trouble. We are never told if God answered Heman's prayers in his lifetime, but we're left to trust that God knew what He was doing. True faith isn't just apathetic acceptance. It is wrestling with the Lord in prayer!

Fifth, *we have an example from God*. Psalm 88 is our invitation to cry out to God in these times. Heman's pain had been poured out before the throne of God, and his requests had been offered. This may have been part of his personal prayer journal. In other words, Heman models for us an acceptable way to bring our pain to the throne of God.

Sixth, *we have comfort from God.* The immediate context of Psalm 88 gives us a clue for our response. God gently cradles the pain and affliction of Heman right between Psalm 87 and 89. Psalm 87 ends, "All my springs are in you!" celebrating the coming reestablishment of Jerusalem as God's earthly throne someday (87:7). Psalm 89, written by Heman's brother Ethan, begins, "I will sing of the steadfast love of the LORD, forever; with my mouth I will make known your faithfulness to all generations" (89:1).

Seventh, *we have the empathy of God.* The fact that Psalm 88, "the saddest Psalm," is even included in Scripture by the Holy Spirit shows that God cares. He understands our pain. He knows what it's like. He doesn't abandon us, even when it *feels* like it. God divinely ordained and composed Heman's words to remind us that He gets it when we suffer!

Psalm 88 doesn't record Heman's comfort and relief after this prayer, but it was most certainly there. God has promised, "Let us then with confidence draw near to the throne of grace, that we may receive mercy and find grace to help in time of need" (Heb 4:16), and Heman was no exception.

The feeling of darkness isn't really darkness at all. It can't be. If you have received Christ as your Savior, having been forgiven of violating God's holy law and character, then you have the spirit of God dwelling within you as the deposit and guarantee of your future inheritance in heaven. If the Spirit of God dwells in you, then you can never be in darkness. "This is the message we have heard from him and proclaim to you, that God is light, and in him is no darkness at all" (1 John 1:5).

15

Joseph Says,
"Expect That God's Wisdom
Will Amaze You"

Depending on how much exposure you've had to systematic theology, you may or may not have heard some big theological words concerning the attributes of God. Some of these words start with the prefix "omni," meaning "all." Most common are "omniscient," meaning "all-knowing," "omnipresent," meaning "all-present," and "omnipotent," meaning "all powerful."

But a less common concept is that God is "omnisapient," that is, all-wise. The omnisapient nature of God says that God uses His perfect knowledge (His omniscience) to omnipotently (with all power) bring about the enactment of His perfect decree. In other words, God makes a perfect plan and has the knowledge and power to make that plan happen.

The concept of God's wisdom overlaps with His other attributes. God's omniscient nature intersects with His omnipotent nature as He perfectly executes the plan He decrees. He declares "the end from the beginning and from ancient times things not yet done" (Isa 46:10). His wisdom says that something is going to happen. His sovereignty makes it happen. And when you put it all together, this is the omnisapient nature of God.

The story of Joseph is one of the most amazing accounts in all the Bible, comprising over 25% of the book of Genesis. From a human standpoint, there is nothing exceptional about Joseph. He was the eleventh of Jacob's twelve sons.

Joseph gives us a long-range look at a man's entire life, from the time he was completely ruined to when he understood the wisdom of God and was able to put the pieces together. In looking at this story and at our own personal trials in life, there are two questions to consider regarding God's wisdom. First, is God wise when great change happens? And second, is God wise when great disappointment happens?

Is God Wise When Great Change Happens?

In the life of Joseph and his brothers, there was always a constant backbone of the family—Jacob. Genesis 37 records that as a seventeen-year-old man, Joseph worked for the family sheep-herding business along with his brothers. The Lord had blessed Jacob with wealth, and his sons were tasked with being good stewards of the flocks and herds. But Joseph's brothers were found to be unfaithful to their task and because of this, Joseph brought a negative report of his brothers to his father Jacob.

Most English Bible translations say that Jacob presented Joseph with a "coat of many colors." Rather than being the multi-colored tunic you might have colored on your Sunday School papers as a child, the traditional phrase actually stems from a set of Hebrew words that literally mean "a robe with long sleeves." But the coat wasn't significant for its colors or even its sleeves. What it *represented* was a foreman's jacket—a public declaration from the father that young Joseph was being promoted to the boss over the family business. Why Joseph? Because his ten older brothers were apparently losing money for their experienced, business-minded father.

As a result of this promotion, Joseph's brothers hated him and "could not speak peacefully to him" (Gen 37:4). However, since they lived in a patriarchal culture where the very worst thing you could do was dishonor and bring pain to your father, they begrudgingly continued on with Joseph in charge. Though the jealousy of Reuben, Simeon, Levi, Judah, Dan, Naphtali, Gad, Asher, Issachar, and Zebulun grew, and though their hatred and disdain for Joseph became more intense, Jacob's presence kept Joseph safe from harm.

The First Great Change

One particular day Jacob sent Joseph to check on the flocks and the men. When the brothers saw Joseph coming from a distance, they plotted how they could kill him and hide his body in an empty cistern. But Reuben, the eldest, turned them from this plan, and convinced them to throw him into the pit alive. Intending to come back for Joseph and "restore him to his father" (37:22), Reuben wanted to keep Joseph alive for his *father's* sake, not Joseph's sake; so again, Jacob's presence kept Joseph alive.

Imagine the feelings of shock and helplessness that your own flesh and blood would turn on you like this and strip you of your foreman's jacket. Imagine the fear in young Joseph's mind as *ten grown men* threw him into a deep, empty cistern, undoubtedly causing physical injury and emotional trauma as their little brother begged and pleaded for mercy. But it gets worse. The text says that the brothers then sat down to eat a meal right above him. Joseph was trapped, unable to climb out of the pit, and he heard his brothers eating, drinking, and talking about their next move. These men had become thugs!

> Then Judah said to his brothers, "What profit is it if we kill our brother and conceal his blood? Come, let us sell him to the Ishmaelites, and let not our hand be upon him, for he is our brother, our own flesh." And his brothers listened to him. Then Midianite traders passed by, and they drew Joseph up and lifted him out of the pit, and sold him to the Ishmaelites for twenty shekels of silver. They took Joseph to Egypt (Gen 37:26-28).

As the story continues, the brothers took Joseph's coat, dipped it in goat's blood, and told their father that Joseph had been torn apart by a wild animal. All this was done to protect themselves. Jacob tore his clothes in lament and put on sackcloth as he mourned and wept for days. The incredible irony is that the brothers lied to protect their own reputation while subjecting their father to a horrifically cruel hoax, and yet they let Joseph live because of their sense of respect for their father. So while they lied enough to cause terrible pain to Jacob, they did not kill Joseph because of the fear of what it might to do to their father. Once again, it was Jacob's influence that kept the family together.

In one of the most familiar and beloved narratives in the Bible, Joseph's life was forever transformed. He became a slave in the house of Potiphar, captain of the Egyptian guard, and eventually rose to the level of chief slave in the house as a type of head butler and household manager. But Potiphar's wife falsely accused him of a crime he didn't commit, and she had him thrown into prison. After several years there, Joseph was given the opportunity to interpret several strange dreams for Pharaoh, king of Egypt. God gave Joseph supernatural wisdom and used him to save the economy of Egypt and the surrounding lands from seven years of devastating famine.

Thirty-year-old Joseph humbly advised, "Let Pharaoh select a discerning and wise man, and set him over the land of Egypt," so that the nation could prepare for the years of famine (Gen 41:33). He proposed to tax the people one fifth of all their produce for the next seven years in order to store up for the seven bad years ahead. Pharaoh agreed with this wise counsel and promoted Joseph from imprisoned slave to "prime minister" over all Egypt. Joseph was now the second most powerful man in the world.

Nine years later, two years into the great famine, Joseph's brothers traveled all the way from Israel to Egypt to buy grain. Through a series of events, Joseph was reunited with his family and, most importantly, with his father. Joseph invited Jacob and the entire family, numbering seventy persons, to the land of Egypt to provide for them. Why was this a big deal? When Joseph finally revealed himself to his brothers after a time of concealing his identity, his first question was, "Is my father still alive?" (45:3). Jacob was still the patriarch, the focus, the center, and the influencing factor that bonded the family together.

It had been over twenty years since that day Jacob had sent Joseph out to the fields to check on his brothers, never to return. At thirty-nine years old, around 1876 BC, Joseph was now reunited with his beloved father. Even though Joseph was extremely blessed by the Lord and had been promoted to a very high position of political and economic power, we cannot underestimate the intense grief he must have experienced during these years. His interactions with his brothers indicate that he loved and missed his family—he was still a son of Israel, and his whole life had been taken from him, turned in a direction he never could have imagined.

The Second Great Change

But now, even after being united with his family for several years, Joseph experienced another life-altering change. Jacob, their beloved father, died. Jacob, the one who had learned what it meant to show grace because of how God had extended it in his own life. Jacob, the one who loved Joseph. Jacob, the father who desired that his boys love each other, the one whom Joseph loved and honored, the one nobody wanted to hurt or disappoint, who had been the glue to keep this family together—had died.

Understanding Joseph's powerful influence in Egypt and afraid of the future now that their father had passed away, the older brothers were terrified. Genesis 50:15 says, "When Joseph's brothers saw that their father was dead, they said, 'It may be that Joseph will hate us and pay us back for all the evil that we did to him.'"

One of the things we as humans grasp for in security is *predictability*. We want to sleep in our own beds, maintain our routines of life, and be able to calmly handle the future with our well-planned schedules and training programs. When a major change comes our way, we prefer to ease into it slowly, giving our hearts and minds time to adjust to the new situation.

But what is often so incredibly painful about suffering is the change that comes fast and without warning. Think about it. You don't get a letter telling you in advance that in a few months you will contract a terminal illness, or lose a family member, or experience a financial crisis. Instead, change often comes out of nowhere, causing grief and anguish. We mourn for the loss of what was and what can no longer be.

In one day, Joseph had gone from being the foreman of the family business to being kidnapped by his family and sold into slavery. Psychologically, this is just about the most horrendous thing that can happen to a person. Joseph's level of hopelessness must have been colossal! Over forty years later, with supposed restoration between Joseph and his brothers, the family experienced massive change as the family patriarch died. What now? Would Joseph have his brothers exiled or even killed?

Is God Wise When Great Disappointment Happens?

Years earlier, in one of the most interesting tests of human integrity, Joseph had put his brothers through a series of examinations to see if they had truly repented and changed. Joseph's brothers first arrived in Egypt to buy grain and stood before Joseph, unaware of who he was. Twenty-two years had passed since they had sold Joseph into slavery—and now their kid-brother was all grown up, living a wealthy, affluent Egyptian life. Who would have thought that this powerful Egyptian ruler was once the helpless young boy whom they had sold to Ishmaelite traders?

However, Joseph recognized them, and when they asked to purchase grain, he roughly accused them, "You are spies!" He presented them with a test to see if he could trust them. They would need to leave one brother in prison and bring their youngest brother, Benjamin, from the land of Israel and from his father's presence to Egypt.

This whole time, Joseph had been speaking the Egyptian language, using an interpreter to communicate with his brothers. He understood Hebrew, but chose not to disclose this fact to the otherwise unsuspecting brothers. Joseph listened carefully as they began to discuss their dilemma amongst themselves. "Then they said to one another, 'In truth we are guilty concerning our brother, in that we saw the distress of his soul, when he begged us and we did not listen. That is why this distress has come upon us'" (42:21).

For the first time in twenty-two years, Joseph heard his brothers acknowledge their sin and say that they were sorry over what they had done. Joseph left the room and wept. For twenty-two years, he thought they had hated him, but now he heard them confess—that's quite a lot to digest!

But Joseph wasn't going to immediately reveal his true identity until he could be sure they were telling the truth. Aware that the famine would last several more years, he sent them back to Israel, knowing they would need to return for more food. He ordered Simeon to be bound before their eyes and taken away to prison, then he gave orders to fill their bags with grain and sent along provisions for the journey. He also secretly put back their own money for the grain in their sacks. When they stopped to rest that night, the men found the money and almost died in fear. What would they do now? How would they be able to face the Egyptian ruler again?

They decided to continue back home, and they told Jacob the whole story. But Jacob refused to send Benjamin back to Egypt to free Simeon. He had lost one of Rachel's sons already and didn't want to lose the other one. Eventually, though, the famine was so bad that they had no choice but to return for more food, this time taking Benjamin with them. In another test of their character and integrity, the brothers returned to Egypt loaded with the money that had been put back in their sacks on the previous trip, money for new grain, as well as extra gifts for Joseph.

When the brothers appeared before Joseph this time, Joseph became emotional at seeing Benjamin, his younger blood brother—the only other son of Rachel and Jacob. Joseph prepared a feast and, much to the amazement of the brothers, arranged their seating places in birth order. Benjamin received *five times* as much food as anyone else during the feast. Normally, the youngest son was barely above the rank of the family dog, but not today! When Joseph sent his brothers away with grain, he again had their money returned to their sacks, but this time he also orchestrated for his own silver cup to be added to the mouth of Benjamin's sack. After they set out for their journey home, Joseph told his soldiers to pursue the travelers and accuse them of stealing his personal cup, revealing the money and the silver cup in Benjamin's bag of grain.

Joseph wanted to know if his brothers had truly repented or if they would allow their youngest brother, Benjamin, to suffer as he had. He wanted to put the brothers back in the same position they had been in with him, over twenty years ago, to see if they had changed. Their little brother, the favored son, was being labeled a criminal, and if declared guilty, he would be taken back to Egypt as a slave, exactly as Joseph had been. How would they respond? Had their hearts softened?

Then Judah stepped forward. He spilled the details of what they had done to their brother Joseph years ago and pleaded that Benjamin be spared, offering his own life instead. Joseph was finally convinced. They had been tormented and truly humbled by their sin. He cried out to his staff, "Get everyone out!" and when he was alone with his brothers, he wept so loudly that the whole household could hear him bawling, saying, "I am Joseph!" What a surprise that must have been for the eleven men standing before him! Joseph told them to go get his father Jacob and bring all the families to Egypt where they could live. Genesis 45:15 says, "And he kissed all his brothers and wept upon them. After that his brothers talked with him."

So they all lived happily ever after, with all relationships completely restored, everyone forgiven, and one big happy family enjoying the Lord's provisions and blessings. Right? Wrong! Seventeen years later, after the family had enjoyed peace and prosperity and Joseph was finally part of the family again, Jacob died and things were about to change again. Joseph was fifty-six, and his ten older brothers had grown up and left the past behind them. All was well... until they *crushed* him with disappointment. His excruciating grief returned as they revealed to Joseph that *they had never really let him back into the family in their hearts.*

> So they sent a message to Joseph, saying, "Your father gave this command before he died: 'Say to Joseph, "Please forgive the transgression of your brothers and their sin, because they did evil to you."'" And now, please forgive the transgression of the servants of the God of your father." Joseph wept when [the messengers] spoke to him (Gen 50:16-17).

These men, who had expressed repentance, now attempted to lie and manipulate Joseph, making up a final wish from Jacob. They demonstrated fear of Joseph instead of filial love and trust. They portrayed themselves as godly men, saying, "please forgive the transgression of the servants of the God of your father," as they simultaneously lied to him (50:17). When the messenger delivered this message to Joseph, he wept bitterly. He had *truly* forgiven them, yet they had kept a fraudulent air about them in fear of him; the restoration had essentially been one-sided. Joseph's disappointment was unimaginable. Seventeen years of family harmony was not what it seemed to be.

One of the great struggles that accompanies suffering and pain is disappointment. And usually the greatest disappointments in life come from those closest to us. We are hurt by those whom we thought were our friends and loved us. This is hard! It feels like pointless pain at times. Like Job, we question, "Are you making me miserable for the sake of being miserable? Does the pain I'm going through right now have a purpose?"

The Answer to Both Questions

Is God wise when great changes happen? Is He omnisapient when great disappointment comes? The answer is an ironic one, but also a truly satisfying one: *Change and disappointment are God's means to bring about stability and joyful satisfaction.* The changes in our lives, however disrupting, actually bring about stability in Christ. The disappointments we experience bring us to satisfaction in God's ultimate plans for our lives!

What good came about from Joseph's tragic circumstances? First, Joseph learned humility. The boy who had once boasted to his family of his high position could now, as the second most powerful man in the world, say, "Am I in the place of God?" For us today, the trials the Lord places before us have an amazing ability to form Christlikeness. We, too, can learn to be humble, but we can also experience joy in the process of being made more like our Savior.

Second, the circumstances of Joseph's teenage years led up to a "restored" relationship once they were reunited. Even though this wasn't exactly true on both ends, it reminds us that what we often long for in the midst of suffering is restoration. But unlike Joseph's situation, we can be confident of a perfect restoration of all things by God, the Creator, because of His perfect and good wisdom.

Third, God used these circumstances years before to set the stage for the ways He would provide for Joseph's entire family years later. Joseph even seems to acknowledge God's common grace to humanity in that many people in the world, besides Egyptian families or even Joseph's family, were saved from starvation through Joseph's influence and leadership. Why could Joseph look back with peace, having been sold into slavery and having his life radically altered? Because he could see the *wisdom* of God at work in sending him ahead to Egypt to one day save his family from starvation. Joseph emulated stability and even joyful satisfaction in seeing God work, even in these incredibly difficult circumstances.

As the saying goes, "When life gives you lemons, make lemonade." When trials and sufferings come, mature Christians understand that it's not that God is the best one who makes lemonade out of lemons. Instead, believers recognize that God put the lemons in their life for a reason—to do something greater than they ever could have imagined.

One of Joseph's most well-known quotes in Genesis is when he told his brothers to not be afraid of what had happened in the past. "As for you, you meant evil against me, but God meant it for good, to bring it about that many people should be kept alive, as they are today" (50:20). Little did he know the depth of this statement or the implications of what it would mean for both his future and for what would happen beyond his lifetime.

Through Joseph's story of great change and disappointment— through the wrecking of a teenage boy's life and family relationships— God's redemptive purposes were at work, setting up for the re-entry of the Jewish nation back into their land, the rebellion of the nation against God, and the eventual coming of the Messiah who would turn what was meant for evil into the greatest good the world would ever know. Joseph had no idea of the scope of God's amazing wisdom!

Take comfort in the fact that not only is God using your suffering for you personally, but also that He is using it for His overarching plan for history. It may not fit into your plan for your life, but it fits perfectly into His. Take comfort in the knowledge that your life and suffering matter— they make a difference! Expect that God's wisdom will amaze you as you remember Romans 16:27, "to the only wise God be glory forevermore through Jesus Christ!"

16

Hannah Says,
"Give Glory to God for His
Gracious Response"

As we have walked this journey together, discovering strength in the river of suffering, I want to remind you of the nature of this river from chapter one:

> We all wade through rivers of tears, but the Lord uses these very rivers to conform us to the image of His Son. They are a gift from the Lord. They may be hard and painful, but they are necessary. Ultimately, we know they are valuable and that they bring peace. The river may be deep and dark and take supernatural fortitude to navigate, but once we are on the other side of that river, we realize that we wouldn't have traded it for anything because of the spiritual value of the trial.[xxvii]

We have examined what men and women in the Bible have to say about a godly response to suffering. Throughout this process we have been asking an underlying question: "How can God be perfectly good if my situation is so *bad*?" This is what theologians call *theodicy*, or as it is sometimes called, "the problem of evil." Personally, I don't care for the phrase "the problem of evil" because it is only a problem from a human standpoint. From this human standpoint, the so-called "problem of evil" says that it is impossible for three facts to exist together:

- God is perfectly good.

- God is perfectly powerful.

- Evil continues to exist.

Human logic says that these three truisms cannot coexist. This could be phrased, "If God is perfectly good and evil continues to exist, then God is not perfectly *powerful* and able to completely prevent evil."[xxviii] Or, "If God is perfectly powerful and evil continues to exist, then God cannot be perfectly *good*." We can't imagine God as less than perfectly good, so we can sometimes, by default, end up concluding that God is doing the best He can but might not always be able to come through in response to a crisis. We would never say that aloud, but our subconscious reasoning may tend in that direction.

However, if you develop a high view of God and a lofty understanding of the scope of His sovereignty—or more accurately, a lofty understanding that you can't fathom the scope of His sovereignty—then with theological confidence, you can say:

- God is perfectly good.

- God is perfectly powerful.

- Evil continues to exist for God's reasons under His total control while He maintains total goodness and power.

If you believe this in theory, the question yet remains: "What about when I, personally, am the one suffering the consequences of evil in the world—even when I have turned to Christ in faith for my salvation?" When a catastrophe on the other side of the world occurs which results in loss of life, I can have sound theology. But what if my wife or husband or child was in that catastrophe? Does my theology remain intact?

Even in the midst of your very worst trial, God is perfectly good and perfectly powerful, and He acts in a gracious manner toward you. Hannah presents the closing argument for this book, showing us the need to give glory to God for His gracious response.

Hannah's Suffering

Hannah lived during the time of the judges in Israel, an era characterized by chaos and disobedience to the Lord. The Book of Judges records a continuous cycle: Israel would turn away from God, be disciplined by God through foreign oppression, cry out for mercy, receive mercy, and be rescued by the Lord. Despite Israel's lawlessness, some individuals still sought the living God with all their heart.

One of these faithful men was Elkanah (1 Sam 1), a Levite who belonged to the honored priestly clan of the Kohathites and who lived with other Levites in the hill country of Ephraim. He was a godly man but, in line with the chaotic confusion and sinful culture of the time, followed the common custom of polygamy. His first wife, Hannah, was the love of his life but could not have children. Since children were essentially a man's retirement plan and were needed to work the family farm or business, it was not uncommon to take a second wife to bear children. So Elkanah married a second wife, Peninnah.

As part of God's plan, Hannah had no children. "The LORD had closed her womb" (1 Sam 1:5). On the surface it appeared that God wasn't showing her favor, and for Hannah this meant agony in the household. Each year Elkanah would take his family to worship the Lord at Shiloh (before Jerusalem had been claimed by Israel and before the temple was built). He showed Hannah favor by giving her double portions of the sacrifice, but a terrible dynamic was at play in the household.

Peninnah "used to provoke her grievously to irritate her" because Hannah could not bear children (1:6). This happened each year as the family went to worship. Peninnah was insinuating that God had forgotten Hannah. We can imagine Peninnah saying, "So, are you *still* praying for a son? Isn't God going to answer your prayers? And by the way, did I tell you? I'm pregnant again!" Year after year, Hannah endured the baiting, tormenting, and irritating insults until she would end up heartbroken, full of tears and unable to eat.

Elkanah had tender love for Hannah, but he wasn't the best at comforting her. He asked, "Hannah, why do you weep? And why do you not eat? And why is your heart sad? Am I not more to you than ten sons?" (1:8). Nice try, Elkanah. He basically said, "Hey, you have *me,* you don't need a son." This was no help at all.

First Samuel 1:8 finds the family at Shiloh once again. At the end of their stay, Hannah was desperate as usual. As Eli, the priest at Shiloh, observed from his seat at the doorpost of the temple, Hannah was "deeply distressed and prayed to the LORD and wept bitterly" (1:10). She vowed to the Lord that if He gave her a son, she would devote the child to Him all the days of his life.

Closing Argument

Hannah takes the witness stand to present one final truth regarding God's character in the river of suffering. In a five-part statement, her story proves the closing argument that even though evil exists and bad things happen, God is still good, and God is still powerful.

God Brings About and Uses Our Suffering

The Lord Himself closed Hannah's womb as a clear indication that this trial was brought on by Him. As the family is in Shiloh to worship, Hannah expresses a desperate, last-minute prayer for a son. Her sorrow remains deep as she has watched Peninnah continue to have babies. In the ancient Israelite culture a woman who couldn't have children was considered to be out of God's favor, since children were a sign of favor from the Lord. But Hannah wasn't desiring children just out of cultural pressure. This was an upright and godly desire given by God.

Psalm 127 had not yet been written in Hannah's day, but certainly the spirit of it was well-known in Israel both culturally and religiously. It expresses that children show God's kindness:

> Behold, children are a heritage from the LORD, the fruit of the womb a reward. Like arrows in the hand of a warrior are the children of one's youth. Blessed is the man who fills his quiver with them! He shall not be put to shame when he speaks with his enemies in the gate (Ps 127:3–5).

Hannah was feeling out of favor with the Lord. As a woman in her time, her identity was tied to having children, and right now she felt useless and rejected. First Samuel 1:10 says she was "deeply distressed." This is one word in Hebrew and is the same root word that Naomi in the Book of Ruth wanted to rename herself: "Mara," meaning "bitterness." The same verse says she "wept bitterly" to the point of having convulsions and physical spasms.

Hannah was experiencing a living death of feeling purposeless. She was suffering immensely, *and this was the Lord's doing.* Consider the irony: Hannah had a good desire given to her by God and God chose to not allow this desire to be fulfilled.

But consider all the good that resulted. This trial was proving the reality of Hannah's faith. The more she suffered, the more she cried out to God. She was learning complete and total dependence on the Lord. She had no choice but to trust the Lord and not her circumstance. By contrast, Peninnah was having babies almost at will, yet displayed no known love for or genuine faith in God. Although Hannah didn't know this at the time, her trial was just the beginning of a plan that would go far beyond her family and would affect the entire nation of Israel. Her trial would end in blessing, not just for her but for countless others as well.

God Brings About and Uses Our Suffering… to Drive Us Humbly to His Purposes

First Samuel 1:11 records Hannah's prayer for a son. She knew the Lord and rightly assumed that the broken heart of an obscure woman from the hill country of Ephraim mattered to God. She determined to take the radical step of promising to give her yet-to-be-conceived son fully to the Lord and that "no razor shall touch his head." She promised to place her son under the vow of the Nazirite as prescribed by the Lord in Numbers 6 so that he would be fully consecrated to God as a full-time servant of the Lord. Hannah's ministry to her future son began in prayer and no doubt continued in prayer throughout the rest of her life.

This humble, God-focused purpose in Hannah represented a change. It was unlikely that when she was first married her prayer would have been such. It would be more likely for a young bride to pray, "Give me many sons that I might be a great woman in Israel!" But as the years passed, her prayers changed. Now her prayer shifted to asking for just one son with the promise that she would give him right back to the Lord for His glory and use. Her prayer for a son was not that he would be handsome, wealthy, and successful, but that God would do with him what He pleased.

Hannah's prayers changed over time from focusing on *her* purpose to *God's* purpose. She was the recipient of God's tender lesson in suffering: suffering aligns our hearts with the Lord's heart and makes us eager to submit to His will. Suffering moves us from wanting to use God for *our* purposes to humbly asking God to use us for *His* purposes.

God Brings About and Uses Our Suffering to Drive Us Humbly to His Purposes... That We Might Return Joyful Thanks to Him

Hannah's prayers were answered, and 1 Samuel 1:20 records the birth of her son. She named him Samuel, meaning "from the Lord." She knew he was God's gift to her and was proud of it. She didn't just say he was God's gift—she really understood and believed it. After Samuel was weaned, Hannah returned to Shiloh "with a three-year-old bull, an ephah of flour, and a skin of wine" (1:24). She brought these gifts as an offering to the Lord out of thankfulness for Samuel, who was about three years old by this time.

Some technical information is necessary to understand the depth of thankfulness in Hannah's heart. There is some debate about the translation of verse 24. The Septuagint,[xxix] the Dead Sea Scrolls, and another major Old Testament text all read "a three-year-old bull." But the Masoretic Text, developed by Jewish scholars between AD 500 and AD 1000 and which has made important contributions to our understanding of the Old Testament, reads "three bulls" instead of "a three-year-old bull." The scholars of the Masoretic Text felt that some older texts interpreted it wrong and uncovered what is called an "intentional scribal error" in which a scribe believed the text to be wrong. In this case, the most likely reason is that three bulls was a small fortune and almost no Jewish family could afford to sacrifice that all at once.

However, according to Numbers 15:8-10, when a person brought *one* bull to sacrifice, they also brought 3/10 of an ephah of flour and about 1/3 of a full wineskin. Hannah brought a full ephah of flour and a full wineskin—*three times* the amount of flour and wine prescribed for a typical one-bull sacrifice. Why? Because she brought three bulls—a *triple sacrifice*. Perhaps Hannah brought a gift to the Lord for each of the three years she got to be with Samuel.

And so, with immense gratitude expressed to the Lord in the form of an extravagant sacrifice, Hannah made an even more extravagant sacrifice: she said goodbye to little Samuel and left him in the care of Eli the priest. She had promised to dedicate the boy to the Lord if He would give her a son and now she was keeping her end of that prayer with a thankful heart.

Her gratitude and joyful thanks comes through in her statement, "Therefore I have lent him to the LORD. As long as he lives, he is lent to the LORD" (1 Sam 1:28). This seems to have the idea of "I have loaned him to the Lord," but the Hebrew word translated "lend" is used 170 times in the Old Testament and is *never* translated "to lend." It is most often translated "to ask" or "to borrow." Hannah had promised to *give* the child to the Lord "all the days of his life" (1:11), not to just *lend* him to the Lord. Verse 28 makes more sense when understood as, "I have *borrowed* him from the LORD." And now she was returning him with overflowing thanks for God's goodness.

Although it may be difficult to feel emotionally at times, whatever trial the Lord brings into your life is meant to impact you so deeply and so positively that you overflow with thanks and gratitude to the Lord. Your trial puts God in His majestic place as King and Sovereign such that any blessing and any mercy that God gives causes a surplus of thankfulness in your heart.

God Brings About and Uses Our Suffering to Drive Us Humbly to His Purposes
That We Might Return Joyful Thanks to Him… To The Exaltation of His Glory

After being blessed with a son, Hannah prayed a prayer of exaltation
(1 Sam 2:1-10). She understood God's grace and demonstrated a stun-
ning grasp of the character of God. In fact, she exalted God's glory, holiness, omniscience, sovereignty, mercy, and justice all in one prayer. First,
Hannah gives full credit and glory to God, saying "my horn is exalted in
the LORD" (2:1). She acknowledges that God alone is her strength, sym-
bolized by the horn.

Then she reminds herself that through God she has victory over
her enemies. The only enemy that Hannah had was Peninnah, but God
showed Hannah favor even over her. Hannah exalts God's uniqueness
and total perfection, stating, "there is none holy like the LORD" (2:2).
In verse 3, Hannah affirms God's omniscient character when she exclaims
that "the LORD is a God of knowledge, and by him actions are weighed."
In verses 4-8, she uses seven word pictures proving God's sovereignty and
His right to do as He pleases:

1. "The bows of the mighty are broken, but the feeble bind on
   strength" (2:4).

2. "Those who were full have hired themselves out for bread, but
   those who were hungry have ceased to hunger" (2:5a).

3. "The barren has borne seven, but she who has many children is
   forlorn" (2:5b).

4. "The LORD kills and brings to life; he brings down to Sheol
   and raises up" (2:6).

5. "The LORD makes poor and makes rich; he brings low and he
   exalts" (2:7).

6. "He raises up the poor from the dust; he lifts the needy from
   the ash heap to make them sit with princes and inherit a seat of
   honor" (2:8a).

7. "For the pillars of the earth are the LORD's, and on them he has set the world" (2:8b).

In verse 9 Hannah celebrates God's mercy, that "He will guard the feet of his faithful ones." Then in verses 9-10 she extols the virtue of God's justice in breaking His adversaries to pieces. Hannah knows her God is a God of glory, holiness, omniscience, sovereignty, mercy, and justice. And in gratitude for God's gift of Samuel, Hannah prays this theological prayer, giving all glory and honor to the Lord.

When you find yourself able to give all glory to God and to be so focused on *His* greatness—His glory, holiness, omniscience, sovereignty, mercy, and justice—then the trial is having the desired impact on your heart and Christlikeness is being worked out in your life. Now your trial is bearing fruit and turns from being a burden to bear to becoming a burden that benefits you.

God Brings About and Uses Our Suffering to Drive Us Humbly to His Purposes That We Might Return Joyful Thanks to Him To The Exaltation of His Glory... For the Totality of His Redemptive Plan

The time of the judges was a transitional time. Israel continued in a state of overall rebellion and chaos. Eli the priest's sons epitomized the spiritual state of Israel in that "the sons of Eli were worthless men" (2:12). They were stealing from the people who came to sacrifice to the Lord and "thus the sin of the young men was very great in the sight of the LORD" (2:17). But Israel had hope. By contrast, "Samuel was ministering before the LORD" (2:18). Unlike Eli's sons, Samuel grew up to reflect his mother's godliness. Each year Hannah would return to Shiloh to visit her son, bringing him a new robe. I can only imagine how tender these annual visits were between mother and son.

Samuel would not just remain the small boy who was Hannah's answer to prayer. Even as a boy God spoke a prophecy through Samuel against Eli, his sons, and Israel as a nation. "And Samuel grew, and the LORD was with him and let none of his words fall to the ground and all Israel from Dan to Beersheba knew that Samuel was established as a prophet of the LORD" (3:19).

Israel went through dark days of the Lord's punishment at the hands of the Philistines, and Samuel, now a strapping young man with the long flowing hair of a Nazirite, gathered the people of Israel.

And Samuel said to all the house of Israel, "If you are returning to the LORD with all your heart, then put away the foreign gods and the Ashtaroth from among you and direct your heart to the LORD and serve him only, and he will deliver you out of the hand of the Philistines" (1 Sam 7:3).

How proud Hannah must have been! God was using Samuel to begin reversing the moral and religious decline of the judges' period to bring Israel back to the relationship they had with God during the time of Moses.

Samuel would act as a judge over Israel and function much like a king. He was the bridge between the wicked time of the judges and the coming time of monarchy, but the people were impatient. Moses had prophetically instructed Israel about their future telling them that they "may indeed set a king over you whom the LORD your God will choose" (Deut 17:15). But Israel's impatience placed Samuel in the role of divinely-appointed disciplinarian. Israel demanded a king from Samuel, not a king in God's timing and in God's power, but a king who, from their perspective, could lead them in battle and make Israel great.

So through Samuel, God gave Israel the king *they* would have chosen: Saul. Saul was a tall and handsome Benjaminite who lacked the character to be God's man. The Lord was gracious and allowed Saul to defeat Israel's enemies for a time, but Saul was a disaster. This king that Israel had so badly wanted made one calamitous and disobedient decision after another. Many times, God sent Samuel to be there to show Saul what should have been done instead. But Samuel's crowning achievement of his ministry happened in the familiar town of Bethlehem. At the Lord's direction, Samuel anointed the true king of Israel, the king of God's choosing: a young boy named David.

What was the big-picture outcome of Hannah's desperate prayer for a son? First Samuel 25:1 records that when Samuel died, "all Israel assembled and mourned for him." Hannah's time of anguish in waiting for a son and then giving him up to the Lord was not just about her. It was part of God's overall redemptive plan for Israel which, of course, includes God's overall redemptive plan for you and me. God made a covenant with the rightful King David. Included in this covenant was a promise that a Davidic King would reign over Israel forever, fulfilled in the most famous of David's descendants, Jesus Christ. God wasn't just working in Hannah's life. He was using Hannah's suffering and His answer to her prayer as part of His overarching plan for all of history: that a Savior would come to die on a cross to pay for the sins of all who would have faith in Him.

In the same way, neither is your suffering ever just about you. God's rich and complex tapestry of sovereign action boasts of wisdom in the interconnectedness of all His dealings. It may be that your suffering has very little to do with you and more to do with how God will use this in the lives of others. This is a wonderful and comforting thought to think that you can be used by God in your most trying hour.

Our closing argument, then, is that *God brings about and uses our suffering to drive us humbly to His purposes that we might return joyful thanks to Him to the exaltation of His glory for the totality of His redemptive plan.* The Lord frequently does more than we ever ask or expect. After the Lord loaned Samuel to Hannah in 1 Samuel 2, He gave her three more sons and two daughters whom she kept for herself!

God is good, and God is powerful. Case closed.

Prayer for the Suffering Saint

My heavenly Father, I accept that Your sovereignty is more vast and infinite than I can ever grasp. I accept that solving my problem should not be my main focus, but I need to willingly submit to Your perfect plan. I trust in Your absolute integrity and ask for the strength to let godly character shine through in the midst of this agony. Help me to find Your power in my weakness. I will plead my cause before You, but I will also praise You no matter what Your answer is. Give me the discipline to obey Your commands and not use my pain as an excuse for sin. Help me to be truly grateful for Your tender care and to find lasting comfort in knowing and trusting You. Help me to give the grace You have given me by forgiving those who have caused my sorrow. Let this season be one of self-examination as I grow more confident in You, even in the darkness. I fully expect that Your wisdom will completely amaze me and, in advance, I give You all glory and honor and praise for whatever gracious response You have ordained. In Jesus, my Savior's name, Amen.

Appendix
15 Days of Strength

In this book, I've presented fifteen lessons gleaned from the experiences of men and women in the Bible. They stand as examples of the faithfulness of God to those who love Him and have been saved by His grace. I wanted to review these lessons with you in a functional format that would enable you to proactively incorporate the lessons into a concentrated time of prayer and right thinking. I encourage you to meditate on each of these lessons and the short devotional that accompanies them, one per day, for fifteen days. I trust that the Lord will minister greatly to your heart as your theology of suffering is bolstered.

Day 1: Accept that God's Sovereignty is Bigger Than You Think

Today, acknowledge to the Lord that His plans are infinitely vast and more than you can possibly grasp. His dealings in your life are not what you have chosen but what He has chosen. And this is important because in the middle of suffering you need God to be as big as He is in reality, not as small and comprehensible as you often wish Him to be. Humble yourself in prayer before a limitless and mighty God and find comfort in His immeasurable control over all things.

Day 2: Solving the Problem
is Not the Point

We desire so desperately for God to just solve our pain and trials, and often He does. But trials give us the opportunity to gain strength in our faith. In fact, without trials, our faith for daily living would atrophy. When you cross over from "solve the problem" territory to "walk through the trial faithfully" territory, there is a breaking-through of peace and patience that only the Holy Spirit can give, which is only given to the child of God in Christ. Although all human efforts may certainly be undertaken to solve the problem, at the same time, remember that the solution is not the point of the trial.

Day 3: Submit Willingly to
the Plan of God

How easy it can be to immediately conclude that God's plan must have taken a day off when our painful situation hit. "God *certainly* would not have meant *me* to go through this—there *must* be some mistake." But your pain *is* part of God's plan, and like every other part of God's plan, your response is simply to submit humbly to Him as even the Lord Jesus Himself did. Great peace is found in submission. In fact, I might even say that you *won't* find peace until you do submit. Acknowledge your humble acceptance of God's all-wise plan, then simply wait upon the Lord. Wait for His timing, His outcomes, and His purposes.

Day 4: Trust in the
Integrity of God

Jesus promised to never leave us or forsake us. He promised to be with us always. He promised to finish the good work He began in us. Therefore, God has not abandoned these purposes. The anguish you find yourself swimming through should *not* put even a small dent in your estimation of the character of God. He will fulfill every promise He has made, and

He will come through for you. When and how is completely His business, not yours, but you *can* trust in God's integrity. Meditate on the complete dependability of God this day.

Day 5: Let Your Godly Character Shine Through

It's tempting to respond to pain with panic, terror, or even sin. Instead, let this be an opportunity to become more mature and refined in your graceful, dignified response to pain. This is not to minimize pain, but rather to decide that the Spirit of God *still* desires to demonstrate the fruit of the Spirit: love, joy, peace, patience, kindness, goodness, faithfulness, gentleness, and self-control. Pray for an elegant and dignified response to pain.

Day 6: Find God's Power in Your Weakness

Ironically, the moment you have no strength left becomes the moment that your trust in the Lord is now involuntary. When you have no emotional strength to bear just one more day, the call of God remains to draw near to Him. This is the moment when you curl up with the Word of God and a cup of tea or coffee and draw immeasurable treasures from the Scripture. When you are weak, then you are strong in the Lord. That is the great paradox of the Christian life. Don't *fight* weakness—*embrace* it.

Day 7: Plead With and Praise the Lord

"Am I supposed to beg God for help or just praise Him and let Him do whatever He is going to do?" The answer is, "*Yes!*" Today, spend time pleading your case to the Lord. Give Him list after list and detail after detail. Plead your cause with all your heart until you can't think of one more single thing to ask of Him. Then, praise the Lord with just as much fervor and pleading as your requests. Thank Him, worship Him, and honor Him. Praise Him that each and every one of the truck-load of requests you just poured out at His feet are going to be heard. Praise Him for Christ and for the gospel and for your salvation. Lift up your voice in thanksgiving and in song. Adore God with your whole being!

Day 8: Obey the Lord in the Midst of Sorrow

Our sorrow and pain so easily and commonly bring forth a sinful response. It can lead us to believe the lie that we are no longer responsible for our tongues, our man-made sinful solutions, or general misbehavior. Joy is never the result of sin, even when you feel that the sin is justified. Quite the opposite happens, as the great joy of a trial can be found in your Spirit-empowered work of responding in righteousness to pain. Be careful not to lash out at those around you, or withdraw from the world, or shirk your responsibilities to your family to the degree that you are physically able to fulfill them. In fact, there is a sense of victory and satisfaction at simply continuing on in persevering obedience to the Lord, growing in His grace each day.

Day 9: Be Grateful for God's Tender Care

No trial is so bad that it could not be worse. As a matter of fact, in the midst of each problem, God weaves in little graces, little blessings. If you begin to count them and look carefully for them, they become a comforting treasure hunt. As you are tempted to see only the black sky, look instead for every star and moon that God shines in the midst of the darkness. These little tender blessings from the Lord provide tangible evidence that He is still walking each and every step with you through the pain and will walk with you across the finish line.

Day 10: God is the Source of Lasting Comfort

We instinctively long for tangible expressions of comfort, for someone who will cry with us and minister to us—someone we can look at and who will be present with us. To be sure, Romans 12 instructs us to weep with those who weep. We are instructed countless times in the New Testament to love one another. This is part of God's plan to strengthen you. But the peace that passes all understanding—the almost indefinable sense that you *are, in fact, going to be okay no matter the outcome*, this remains God's alone to give you. Sit at His feet counting on your Lord to breathe fresh hope into your heart. God alone can make the ash heap of Job be a place of true lasting comfort.

Day 11: Humbly Forgive Those Who Have Caused Sorrow

In many cases, your suffering will include grief at the hands of another. When this person is close to you, the anguish is almost unbearable. Most people I have counseled through suffering indicate that they would rather deal with an inanimate problem, such as a disease or financial crisis, than deal with the unspeakable pain of a breaking or broken relationship. But the mandate from Christ in Luke 17 and from Paul in Ephesians 4 is clear that, as forgiven people, we are to forgive. This simply means that you need to apply the same grace God gave you toward the one who has hurt you. You are no more deserving of salvation than they are. Today, forgive and pray for your enemies.

Day 12: Use Your Suffering for Self-Examination

The age-old argument as to whether or not the Lord is disciplining you in your pain is really an irrelevant argument. The Lord disciplines those whom He loves, and He loves you. Therefore, all believers experience the

Lord's kind, fatherly discipline. What sins have continually plagued you? With whom do you need to make amends relationally? Where have you not been as faithful and diligent as you should be pleasing to the Lord? What bitterness and anger have you harbored? How could you be a better husband, wife, father, or mother? What admonitions from others have you repeatedly ignored and snubbed? Use this day to answer some of these tough questions, and ask the Lord to grow you in maturity.

Day 13: Be Confident in the Lord's Presence in Darkness

Darkness is a common metaphor for a painful situation. In fact, darkness and depression has a physical component to it. You can feel as if something is tangibly on your shoulders. You can feel tired and apathetic. Darkness has a palpable quality to it. And the worst part about darkness is the temptation to simply believe that God has abandoned you because you can't see Him working. The darkness clouds your vision of God in your trial. But He is there. He never left, and He never will. In fact, He is holding your hand for each and every careful step through the darkness. Find comfort and confidence today in God's abiding presence.

Day 14: Expect That God's Wisdom Will Amaze You

Take an imaginary time machine and go forward in time to the end of your trial. It may be a month, a year, a decade, or even perhaps not until you go home to heaven. But once you arrive, get out of the time machine and look back. Look at God's solution, at all the good that came from the trial, and at all the blessings you and others received as a result. I guarantee that what you will see will make you shout for joy and amazement. In fact, I believe that blessing will be so immense that, knowing what you now know, you would choose to experience the trial all over again just to get that tremendous blessing. The time machine idea is not mine; in fact, it is biblical. The wanderer Abraham who lived in tents in a foreign land "was looking forward to the city that has foundations, whose designer and builder is God" (Heb 11:10).

Day 15: Give Glory to God for His Gracious Response

Ultimately, the most important reaction to pain that you are to have is to worship God. In every moment of your trial God did exactly the right thing, and He did all things for His glory and for our benefit. The most crucial result of your torment and affliction needs to be that you are a significantly better worshiper of God. Your knees should be worn from prayer. Your face should be dirty from bowing before Him. Your eyes should be filled with tears, not just at your pain but at God's immense and awe-inspiring glory. All that the Lord has done in your life is gracious. Yes, this even includes sorrow. Meditate on the fact that God is gracious and kind in all He does for you.

May you find strength in your river of suffering until that day when the only river you know is "the river of the water of life, bright as crystal, flowing from the throne of the God and of the Lamb" (Rev 22:1).

Endnotes

i   Originally rendered "YHWH"

ii   Osteen, Victoria. <http://www.victorioaosteen.com/pages/Family.aspx> February 12th, 2015.

iii   F. B. Huey, *Jeremiah, Lamentations,* vol. 16, The New American Commentary (Nashville: Broadman & Holman Publishers, 1993), 475.

iv   John Piper, "Ten Aspects of God's Sovereignty in Suffering and Satan's Hand in It" in *Suffering and the Sovereignty of God,* ed. John Piper and Justin Taylor (Wheaton: Crossway Books, 2006), 18.

v   John L. Mackey, *Lamentations,* Mentor (Geanies House, Fearn, Tain, Ross-Shire: Christian Focus Publications, 2008), 153.

vi   Names are not used to protect the privacy of the family.

vii   Authuer Bennett, ed., *The Valley of Vision: A Collection of Puritan Prayers and Devotions* (Edinburgh: The Banner of Truth Trust, 1975), 101.

viii   Allen P. Ross, *Creation and Blessing* (Grand Rapids: Baker Books, 1998), 400.

ix   http://www.awmi.net/extra/article/authority_releases (accessed 3-28-15)

x   Murray J. Harris, *The Second Epistle to the Corinthians: A Commentary on the Greek Text,* New International Greek Testament Commentary (Grand Rapids, MI; Milton Keynes, UK: W.B. Eerdmans Pub. Co.; Paternoster Press, 2005), 858.

xi   http://www.desiringgod.org/articles/don-t-waste-your-weaknesses-
      in-2014 (accessed 3-28-15)

xii   https://www.goodreads.com/author/quotes/3715.Joni_Eareckson_
      Tada (Accessed 6-27-2016). Full citations for each quote can be found
      at this site.

xiii http://www.columbia.edu/~js322/misc/hus-eng.html (Accessed
      4-17-2015)

xiv   Tacitus, *The Annals of Imperial Rome* cited in "The Burning of Roma,
      64 AD," Eyewitness to History, www.eyewitnesstohistory.com (1999).

xv   http://crossexamined.org/what-really-happened-at-nicea/ (accessed
      4-24-2015)

xvi   Cited in Matt Woodley, *The Folly of Prayer: Practicing the Presence
      and Absence of God.* I make no endorsement one way or another of
      Woodley's book. But the quote from Bayly is thought-provoking.

xvii http://www.huffingtonpost.com/2014/04/26/scents-and-
      wellbeing_n_5193609.html (accessed 5-2-2015)

xviii http://alinenewton.com/neuroscience-of-touch-touch-and-the-brain/
      (accessed 5-2-2015)

xix   Name has been changed to protect the privacy of the family.

xx   Charles H. Spurgeon, "The Panting Hart," Metropolitan Tabernacle
      Pulpit, vol. 14, (London: Passmore and Alabaster, 1869; reprint ed.,
      Pasadena, Tex.: Pilgrim Publications, 1982), 417.

xxi   R. Kent Hughes, *Beginning and Blessing* (Wheaton, IL: Crossway,
      2004), 53.

xxii R. Laird Harris, "The Mist, the Canopy, and the Rivers of Eden,"
      Bulletin of the Evangelical Theological Society, unspecified issue,
      1968.

xxiii http://soniamarsh.com/2011/09/are-women-divorcing-for-frivolous-
      reasons.html (accessed 5-23-2015).

xxiv http://www.telegraph.co.uk/women/mother-tongue/8739533/
Women-and-divorce-Goodbye-darling-youre-just-too-dull....html
(accessed 5-23-2015).

xxv http://psychcentral.com/blog/archives/2011/01/15/9-types-of-hope-
lessness/ (Accessed 6-3-2015).

xxvi Ibid.

xxvii Page 15

xxviii This is the basic position of the theological view Open Theism.

xxix Greek translation of the Old Testament